CONVERSATIONS FROM THE COUCH

CONVERSATIONS FROM THE COUCH

DEMYSTIFYING THE THERAPEUTIC EXPERIENCE

LOUISE VAN DER EIJK

To all of my clients
past and present
You teach me something new
every day

the experience
the ache of being human
no one can escape

CONTENTS

CONVERSATIONS FROM THE COUCH

Cover Created by Teaberry Creative - Adobe Firefly Image

Publishing Services provided by Stacey Smekofske @ Print To Pro

Published by GYST Wellness

The author has attempted to recreate events, locales, and conversations from memory. To maintain anonymity names of individuals and places have been changed. Identifying characteristics and details such as physical properties, occupations, and places of residence may also have been changed.

This publication is meant as a source of valuable information for the reader; however, it is not meant as a substitute for direct expert assistance. If such a level of assistance is required, the services of a competent professional should be sought.

If you are in crisis or need immediate support, please contact the Suicide & Crisis Lifeline by calling or texting 988 (US) or reach out to a local mental health service in your area. Help is available.

Library of Congress Control Number: 2025910356

Paperback: 978-1-968191-00-9

Hardback: 978-1-968191-01-6

eBook: 978-1-968191-02-3

A NOTE FROM THE AUTHOR

Since beginning my work as a counselor in 2007, I noticed that over the years many themes and conversations seemed to return again and again. Everyone is unique, but many challenges faced by individuals are shared by others. This book was born out of those recurring themes. I wanted to capture my observations and share them with you, and show you what therapy often reveals: that many of the struggles we think isolate us are, in fact, universal and collectively experienced.

Dr. Louise van der Eijk

1

THE IMPORTANCE OF VALIDATION

The great Carl Rogers (1902-1987), founder of humanistic and client-centered counseling, identified that rapport is essential for the counseling process to work. It has been identified that the single biggest contributor to a client's success and progress in a therapeutic setting is the rapport they build with the therapist.

Rogers established three main characteristics that help build rapport in the counseling process. These are acceptance, genuineness, and empathy. He believed it was essential for counselors to fully accept the client for who they are, including their emotions and their responses to the events in their lives. When a therapist fully accepts the client for who they are, the client feels safe opening up and talking about their deepest thoughts and feelings.

> Acceptance, genuineness, and empathy.
> Three simple words,
> one powerful transformation.

With genuineness, Rogers refers to the counselor's emotional response toward the client. When the client feels that the counselor is genuinely concerned, instead of fake concerned, or the therapist's responses are real, this increases the sense of safety for the client.

Empathy refers to the ability to see things from another person's perspective. It's about putting aside one's beliefs and values and fully placing oneself in another person's shoes to see things from their perspective.

In essence, Rogers believed in validating the client's experience, and I completely agree. In my years as a therapist, I have come to see that people thrive on validation, and people genuinely want to be heard.

Validating someone in your life is about allowing them to have their own emotional experience. It's about letting them know that they are allowed to feel whatever they're feeling and that the simple fact of their emotions makes their experience right. There is no wrong way to feel. If something causes you to be upset, then guess what? You're allowed to be upset!

This sounds like a pretty basic concept, but unfortunately, this is not easily understood. One common misconception is that when someone else feels something different from you, and what you feel is right, the other person's feelings must be wrong. Well, newsflash, buddy! You both can have opposite feelings about something, and you can both be right!

Your feelings and thoughts are right for you, and someone else's feelings and thoughts are right for them. You don't get to decide on what someone else ought to be feeling. This is an accumulation of a lifetime of experiences, beliefs, values, lessons, personality differences, etc., and no two people have had the same life. When someone else has a different emotional experience than you, so be it. They are as right as you are in your feelings.

A pattern we get caught up in is believing feelings are an objective, scientific, or right or wrong thing. Ultimately, they stem from values, and when it comes to values, there isn't a right or wrong. Values give priority to some things and identify what is more important and what is less important. We often try to break these down into universal principles, but why this usually leads to conflict is that by doing so, somebody else's values are deemed wrong.

This is probably one of the most recurring forms of conflict in couples. I see this happen frequently. One side of the couple is unable or unwilling to see the other person's side. Many people get stuck in black-and-white thinking and see the world as either right or wrong, not realizing that many rights can coexist, even if they appear opposite.

We all experience the world through a very subjective lens. Everything we see is perception, and yes, matter and things existing in the world are the same for all of us, but we are looking at the same thing, but that doesn't mean we see the same thing.

Even though we don't need validation to survive, we inherently feel better when we're validated. When you're at your job and you're doing what needs to be done, not necessarily working harder and doing what's in your job description, and then your boss comes along and thanks you for doing a good job, stating that he values you as an employee, the act makes you feel better and perhaps even makes you want to work a bit harder. We don't need validation, but we become nicer people when we both give and receive validation.

A common criticism I encounter comes when I encourage people to validate others. They will ask why they should validate someone when they're doing what they're supposed to be doing, anyway. My answer is that the validation builds connection, trust, safety, and security, and encourages that individual to do even better. It makes them feel closer to you. Quite often, when validation is received, it is then reciprocated. Do you want to feel encouraged and supported by someone in your life? Encourage and support them first, and you may be surprised by the response.

The most effective discipline/parenting style is positive reinforcement. I've had discussions with people who say positive reinforcement is bribery or pro-social manipulation. These may look similar on the surface, but it is distinguished by the intent behind the actions. The intention behind positive reinforcement is to teach good behavior. Through conditioning, children (and animals!) learn that it is more desirable to engage in certain behaviors over others, as these behaviors will be rewarded. The intention is to teach discipline, set limits, and help individuals become emotionally regulated adults.

Pro-social manipulation includes the word **manipulation**, which has a negative connotation. The connotation of the word manipulation is swindling someone else's behavior for one's selfish gains. This is relevant to bribery, which is manipulating a person's response or actions for personal gain. So even though the gist of the behavior looks the same (if you do this, then you'll get this out of it), the intent behind the action is very different. Even with bribery, the reward is usually not positive, but instead it is the prevention of an unwanted outcome (e.g., if you do this for me, I won't leak those pictures I have of you).

When you validate someone, you're not being weak, vulnerable, mushy, or whatever other defense you may have about lifting someone up. Validation helps build relationships, and everyone could use a bit more of this in their lives!

Here's another important thing to know about validation: you can validate someone even while disagreeing with them. Validating someone's experience and allowing them to feel what they are feeling doesn't mean you have to feel it, too. For example, if someone tells a joke and one of you thinks it's funny, but the other is offended by the joke, it doesn't mean that one of you is wrong. The offended person's feelings are as valid. Something in their experience has been triggered, and this feeling is as valid. Applying empathy and working toward understanding this person's perspective can help you validate their experience of being offended, even if you still believe the joke is funny. You may not agree that something is offensive and, at the same time, validate the fact that someone was offended. These feelings and actions can coexist. Again, feelings are not right or wrong; they are. Maybe I should say that feelings are not wrong or wrong; they are always right. Whatever you're feeling, it is right for you. You can validate someone's experience while at the same time not agreeing with it.

Validating someone else's experience doesn't mean you're giving up your viewpoint or experience about it. Once again, there is room for both (or all) feelings and perspectives to exist at the same time. When you validate someone, you're simply allowing them to have their experience without necessarily needing to change it or to get them to change their position to your (emotional) experience. I can tell you right now, when you validate someone's experience, they're going to be much more willing to validate yours. Funny how that works.

"Yes, but surely, it's not right for someone to hurt someone else out of anger, so why should this be validated?"

Why, thank you. I'm so glad you brought this up.

When it comes to validation and allowing others to have their experience about it, it's important to distinguish between thoughts, feelings, and behaviors. Thoughts, feelings, and behaviors are completely different things, and while it's important to validate feelings, sometimes behaviors are not okay.

Whatever you're feeling, whether it's anger, anxiety, doubt, resentment, or excitement, you're entitled to feel it. However, this doesn't mean that acting on it is always okay. Emotions are what we feel, but actions and behaviors are things that we do. This is an important distinction. In the end, we can think whatever we want to think and feel whatever we're feeling, but there are consequences to our actions.

I can be completely angry at someone, and justifiably so, but does that give me the right to punch them in the face? Absolutely not! I can feel hurt over the actions of another and feel resentment and anger, but does that give me the right to retaliate? Also no. You are allowed to express your feelings, but that doesn't give you the right to act inappropriately.

You can feel something and act with polite restraint. Both of these things can coexist. For example, I can work with a difficult colleague and feel frustrated in their presence, and still be nice to them. I can feel full after eating a large meal, but when a delicious dessert is presented,

I can still eat some more. Because I feel a certain way doesn't mean I have to act on it. I can feel angry at someone and want to punch them in the face, and still not punch them in the face. Feelings and behaviors are two different things. Because one exists does not mean the other has to follow.

Validation helps us work toward building an understanding of what is driving certain behaviors rather than judging the same behaviors, and this can have a huge and positive impact on relationships. If a child is struggling in school, instead of judging them for being lazy or not working hard enough, validation will allow us to recognize that this child's experience is to struggle and wonder why they are struggling, instead of criticizing.

If someone is angry, one of our first responses is to get defensive. However, if we showed a level of empathy and worked to understand why they were angry, we might reach a resolution much quicker.

Empathy starts when we stop trying to win and start trying to understand.

Many years ago, when I was working at a community mental health clinic, a client came in very upset and was rude to the front desk staff. Attempts to calm him down were not successful, so I was called to help. First, I considered that this individual had a reason to be upset, so I worked on exploring why he was so upset. He said that he'd been in for a prescriber appointment at our clinic earlier that day, and when he went to pick up this prescription at the pharmacy, his insurance did not cover it. He was very upset because he needed this medication and felt it was bad practice for the prescriber to prescribe something he couldn't get. I remember telling him, "You know, I also would be upset if that happened to me." Upon hearing this, his disposition changed because, at that moment, he knew I was on his side. We were able to sort the situation out, and he left feeling validated. He could have easily been sent away with the message that his aggression was unacceptable and to come back when he was calm, but validating his experience diffused the situation.

If we can explore the reason for unhealthy behaviors and validate a person's need (feeling) to act the way they are (validating their emotions, not the behaviors), then we fill their need to feel heard and encourage healthier behavior.

An example of validation and encouraging better behavior can be when dealing with a school bully who feels the need to boss others around. I once worked on a scenario when a bully's behavior was often condemned, as it should be, but condemning it didn't change the behavior. When the teacher applied empathy and questioned why this young boy felt the need to act in such an aggressive and controlling way, the teacher learned that the boy had no control over his own life. His parents were bordering on being emotionally and verbally abusive. The boy felt like the only time he had any control over his own life was when he controlled others. Once the teacher understood, they gave him small assignments, helping him feel in charge of different things, such as going around the room to collect everyone's homework or wiping the board after a lesson was finished. These small tasks gave the boy a sense of leadership, and his behavior was positively reinforced. The teacher told him that he was becoming a role-model to others, which gave him the feeling that others were looking up to him. He was influencing others, giving him a sense of control. His bullying behaviors lessened, and he found positive ways to fulfill his needs.

When we can sit still long enough to explore underlying motives for behaviors, we go on to find ways to meet needs in healthier ways.

2
THE BRAIN AND EMOTIONS

Let's talk about what happens in the brain when we become emotional, including when we become angry and impulsive. I think that sometimes it's easier to change behaviors or apply certain behaviors if we know why and how something works instead of changing because we are told to.

For example, if I'm incredibly mechanically naive, and I buy my first car, and the car dealer tells me to change the oil every 3000 miles, I may think, "Okay, great! I have no idea why, but they told me to do it. Okay, I suppose I'll do that." I drive the car about 3000 miles and then realize it's time to get an oil change. So, I get an oil change. And then another 3000 miles roll around, and then I get another oil change. The engine feels good, and it sounds good. I continue to drive my car, and it feels great, but another 3000 miles roll around and I think, "Why do I need to get an oil change? Everything sounds good, everything feels good, and the car feels good. I'll drag this oil change out a bit, and maybe around 4000 miles, I'll get an oil change." Things might go well for a while, but I might be pushing my luck. If that same car dealer told me that it's important to change the oil every 3000 miles and instead said, "Here, let me show you what happens in the engine if you don't get regular oil changes. When the oil gets old, the engine doesn't work so well."

If the mechanic explains to me what's going to happen in my engine and maybe even shows me some things, or compares an engine that hasn't had an oil change to a well-maintained engine, I will be more inclined to get that regular oil change! So, at 3000 miles, I think to myself, my engine feels good and sounds good, but I'm going to get that oil change because I know what's going to happen if I don't!

Like that mechanic being more clear in their instruction, I find that changing behavior is easier when a person understands some of the workings of the brain when we become emotional. It helps to know what is physically going on.

The brain consists of many parts and regions: the occipital lobe, the parietal lobe, the cerebral cortex, the prefrontal cortex, the limbic system, and the brain stem. The brain stem is often referred to as the lizard brain; a lot of our instincts and fears come from there, including our fight-or-flight response. The automated parts of us respond from the brain stem.

The limbic system is in the middle of our brain, and a component of the limbic system is the amygdala. This is the emotional processing center of the brain. When something happens to us, and then we feel an emotion, that emotion is processed in the limbic system.

For example, say that you and I witness an event, and something happens, and I get angry about what happened. That's because the limbic system in the brain is processing the situation and provides that response. Now, you might see the same event and think it's hilarious, so for you, the limbic system might invoke some kind of joy or positive response. Even though we see and experience similar things, we process our responses differently. Our emotional responses originate in the limbic system.

The front part of the brain includes the prefrontal cortex, and out of all the animal species, the human prefrontal cortex is the most developed. The prefrontal cortex sits in our forehead and is responsible for things like logic, reasoning, and analysis. It makes sense that in humans, this is the most developed because we're the only species that can access foresight to the extent that we do. We're also the only species that has the level of consciousness that we have–we know that we know.

For example, we can reason. If I do this, it's going to lead to this, so I'm going to do this because it will lead to this. Or, if I do this thing now, then I can do this other thing later. So, we have this ability to think ahead and plan ahead.

We sometimes choose our careers back in high school and know that if we study and get a degree in a particular subject, go to that particular school to pursue an education, then that's going to help us ten years from now. We can plan ahead and project how today's actions will affect us many years from now. This also goes for spending. If I save money, then I'll be able to buy something nice with it later, but if I spend it all now, I won't be able to.

We can plan and reason, and of course, there are a lot of different types of analyses and logical deductions controlled by the prefrontal cortex. For example, math, science, and following IKEA instructions to put that table together! Even recipes necessitate us to follow instructions and measure ingredients. Your prefrontal cortex helps you solve a little science formula, but with tastier results. It's an analytical process, nonetheless! I don't know about you, but I don't know any other species that can put a bunch of different ingredients together and make an elaborate meal.

The prefrontal cortex (which is responsible for logic, reason, and analysis) and the limbic system (the emotional processing center of the brain) are constantly communicating and networking with each other. Neurons are firing. There are whole networks of communication happening between those two centers of the brain, and our brains are all wired together, allowing them to communicate through neural pathways.

Your brain isn't stuck.
It's rewiring every time you choose differently.

For example, if someone does something that causes me to feel upset, then my feelings are determined by the limbic system. It processes the anger and recognizes that something's happening, leading me to feel my emotional response. But because my limbic system is communicating with the prefrontal cortex–my reasoning and logic–I also have the foresight to know that how I deal with this anger will determine the consequences I will potentially face.

If I say okay, let me take a few deep breaths and let me figure out what I want to say to this person, then I know that this response is going to have better consequences because I will not hurt myself or others in the process. I might want to be able to maintain a relationship with this person. So, even though I'm feeling angry, my prefrontal cortex can logically assess what I'm going to do and how to react.

Now, another response could think, "Man, I want to punch this person in the face! That would feel so good right now!" So the limbic system might concur and get excited because punching the person in the face would be a great feeling. "Let's do that!" But because my limbic system is communicating with the prefrontal cortex, my reasoning kicks in and says, "Now, wait a minute! Let's apply some logic and analysis to this. If I punch this person in the face, I might get into a fight that is going to end up worse for me. I could get arrested and lose this friendship forever." That's a lot of possible consequences that I may not be willing to risk. Therefore, I could decide not to punch the person in the face.

Why is it, then, that sometimes we do act on emotions, and we don't seem to have that rational response at that time? Well, even in this scenario, there's something else going on in the brain. When emotions are extremely heightened, or when we're used to acting on impulse, the limbic system and the prefrontal cortex stop communicating.

You probably have seen this or experienced it yourself. For example, some people claim to have blackout rages and don't remember anything about their angry outbursts and related behaviors. It's like they go into an altered state. It's in those scenarios that the limbic system and the prefrontal cortex are no longer communicating.

This also happens with individuals who are familiar with acting on impulse and have never had consequences that caused them to slow down and change their behavior. This can stem from early childhood. For example, if discipline and punishment were also met with heightened emotional responses instead of logic and reason, maybe the child's parent would yell and scream at them or react with violence. In cases involving abuse, a child doing something wrong could invoke a heightened emotional and impulsive response from the parent instead of the parent opting for a teaching moment about their child's behavior needing to be changed.

The behavior of someone who repeatedly reacts without employing logic is often role-modeled. If a child witnesses a lot of violence or anger outbursts from their parents, the child learns that the behavior is how problems are dealt with and responded to.

A healthier response allows neural pathways and communication to grow between the limbic system and the prefrontal cortex, teaching children to think more about consequences and add reason to how they respond to their emotions. The child would instead think, "If I hurt someone and my mom or dad sits me down to have a conversation about what I did, I have to think about that." The child would have to apply their limited logic and reasoning to understand what consequences their actions caused. In this scenario, using the prefrontal cortex forces the limbic system to communicate, making the neural pathways stronger.

Some people don't learn how to do this. This may come from poor role-modeling and poor parenting, but when people constantly act on their emotions, they can give up because they feel that they can't deal with the situation. After all, the emotions are too high. The neural connections and the pathways between the limbic system and prefrontal cortex weaken, and it then becomes easier to act on impulse and harder to reason and follow difficult situations through in a rational manner.

When someone acts on their urges without thinking it through, the limbic system and the prefrontal cortex stop communicating, and the individual doesn't have a logical and reasoning thinking capacity because this part of the brain is disconnected.

We all know someone, or maybe yourself, who has acted on impulse and made very questionable decisions and, after the fact, wonders, "What was I thinking?" Well, you weren't! You acted in a heightened emotional state, and your reasoning capacity wasn't available. This is why it's easy to act on impulse, and why it's so hard to manage impulses when they're happening. There's a disconnect that's happening in the brain.

There is good news, though. You can retrain your brain. Our brains are these amazing computers in our bodies, and they're capable of doing some amazing things.

In one of the more recent discoveries about the brain, the phenomenon of neuroplasticity was uncovered. This essentially refers to the ability of the brain to mend itself and rewire itself, and this can happen at any age in a lifetime. The common belief was that around the early twenties, the brain stopped developing, but actually, this isn't true.

There's been a ton of research on neuroplasticity and how we can lose certain parts of brain functioning, and a different part of our brain will take over and take on the responsibilities of the lost functioning. So, our brains are constantly changing and developing. This never stops! There's a lot of amazing literature on neuroplasticity and this phenomenon, so I'm not going to take up a lot of space on it here, but it is important to point out that you can rebuild and strengthen those neural connections and pathways between the limbic system and the prefrontal cortex.

If you feel you are very impulsive and you don't feel in control of your impulses, you now know that you can learn how. One of the best ways to manage impulsivity is to engage in breathing exercises. As soon as you find that you're feeling impulsive and your emotions are high, or you feel like you want to act on these impulses, make your default response to take a few deep breaths.

When you activate mindful breathing, your limbic system, which is fired up and has stopped connecting with the prefrontal cortex, will settle down and reconnect. You can then make more rational decisions about what you're going to do with whatever emotions you're currently feeling.

Mindful breathing
is a reset button for your brain.

Like with the car mechanic teaching *why* an oil change is important rather than that it is, when you understand what is happening in the brain, you're more likely to put skills in place to manage impulsivity. It helps to recognize and implement some of the skills, such as breathing skills and other mindfulness skills, to help build your neural pathways, and then you're making your reasoning capacity a lot stronger. Once you make this a habit, it will be a lot easier for you to be able to experience your emotions and stay rational.

There's a saying in neuroplasticity: "Neurons that fire together, wire together," and that's exactly what is happening. Whenever you don't act on an impulse but instead take a few deep breaths, pause to ask yourself what you want to do with the emotions you're feeling.

Consider the most effective way to handle the situation that caused you to be upset. Each time you practice this, you're building new pathways. You're allowing new neurons to fire together, and you're making the wiring stronger.

Think of the following analogy. You live in a house, and there's a huge field between your house and the town. Whenever you go to a store in town, instead of going all the way around the field, you walk across the field because it's much shorter and more convenient. Now, the very first time you cross this field to go to the store and then get home again by going through the field again, you look back at the field, and there's no change; it looks the same as before you went to the store. Well, soon you need to go to the store again, so you go. You cross the field again, and you walk the same way through the field because it's the most direct line to the store. Then you go home again, you look at the field again, and still there's no change.

However, over the years, if you do this time after time, every time you go to the store and you come back and you use the same route, guess what's going to happen to the grass? You're going to start making a path in the grass, and then it's going to be a lot easier for you to use this path. The more you do something, the more ingrained it becomes, literally, as in the field, but this is exactly what happens in the brain as well.

When you have a certain behavior, and you constantly default to this behavior, you're making that neural pathway a lot stronger because that's your default response. If your default response is to act on anger and impulse, then that will be easy for you to default to because you've built those neural pathways so strongly. In the beginning, it might be challenging for you to behave differently because of those neurons that have been wired and firing together for so long.

Now imagine that you're back in your house by the field, and the store has moved to the other side of town. You need to walk a different path across the field to get to the store. You still need to walk across the field, but in a whole new direction. So now you need to remember to walk the other way. It could even happen that a few times you start walking down your old path, and you realize the store has moved to the other side of town. Then you need to backtrack and go the other way because your default response was to walk down the path you've been using for years. Using the path was your automated response.

Over time, you get used to the store being in a different place, and you start to walk the new path. Like the old path, if you walk the new path repeatedly, then over time, you will make a new path in the grass. The same thing happens in the brain when you implement a new behavior. It's probably very challenging in the beginning, but through repetition, the neural pathway grows stronger, like the path in the field.

When you stop using the old path because it no longer serves a purpose, the grass will grow over it. It may take a while, but over time, that old path is going to be completely covered up. You're going to be left with one path that you can see in the field, which is the new path. This is also what happens in the brain.

I want you to take from this chapter the understanding of what happens in the brain with an emotional response and how your wiring influences the response you choose. By having a better understanding of what is happening in the brain, it might be easier for you to implement changes and understand why that's important.

As you're implementing changes in how you respond to emotions, you're also learning how changing the wiring in your brain makes those new behaviors easier.

3
ALL FEELINGS ARE VALID

When clients come into my office, they are struggling with all sorts of different things. Nobody comes to counseling because things are going well, and they want to talk about the good stuff. Of course, I'm exposed to a lot of the negative side of life, but one of the things I think is important to emphasize is that with all the negative things that happen in our lives, there's a place for that.

There's a lot of emphasis on having to change things that happen or change our feelings because we're not supposed to feel bad, or that the emotions that don't feel good are bad. Even with experiences that we have, like struggles and adversities, there's an emphasis on needing to turn these around, and every day has to be a great day. We should be positive every day. If we're having a bad day or we're in a bad mood, we must turn that frown around.

One of the things that we haven't learned to do as humans is to sit with the bad stuff and hold a place for that in our lives. It's great to strive for positive things and work toward your goals. However, it's also important to recognize that where you are is also important. Even though you want things to be better, it's important to acknowledge the present moment. There's room for both to coexist.

For example, if you strive to be nicer to people, and you've been irritated, stressed, and grumpy, and you have a lot of things on your mind, you might tell yourself that you'll be a nicer person when you treat others more kindly. This, of course, is okay, but at the same time, don't forget to value who you are today, even with your irritability, even with your stress, because that is also part of the human experience.

> Your emotions—all of them—
> are part of the human experience.
> Not just the happy ones.

This is one of the beautiful things I have to remind myself of when I counsel people. I see my clients upset, crying, retelling, and reliving trauma, and all the emotions that they're experiencing are part of the human experience.

I believe there's so much value in making room for all emotions, and we can remind ourselves that everything that we experience is part of the human experience, not just the good stuff.

For example, one of the big negative emotions or negative experiences that we go through, which is very much a human experience, is grief. A lot of times, when people experience grief, they're told positive things, such as "they're in a better place," or "they're no longer suffering." And while these statements can be incredibly comforting, it's also okay to acknowledge the loss and feel those emotions that don't feel good.

I believe that when you remind yourself that the more intensely you feel any given emotion, the more you're having a human experience, because the range of emotions that we experience is ultimately all human.

I know that animals feel emotions, too, and they have expressions of emotions, too. I know that when my dog Indigo was a lot younger and had a lot more energy, one of her little antics she would pull was to rummage through the trash. There'd be trash everywhere, all scattered through the house, and I'd come home from work and look at her, then point to a piece of trash and ask her, "What's this?" Immediately, she would have a guilty expression on her face, and sometimes, she wouldn't even look at me! She knew she was guilty, and I know every dog owner can relate to this story!

Other animals experience excitement, joy, and sadness, but I believe the range of human emotions is far more complex. It's part of the human experience to go through all of it.

One of my biggest experiences throughout my career was working a contract in the Oregon Department of Corrections, which I did for four and a half years. Very consistently, with the inmates that I worked with, it was part of their instinct to suppress any kind of emotion that they would feel, even joy and excitement, but especially the emotions that didn't feel good, like sadness. Even expressions of gratitude or providing validation or support to others were also suppressed.

Some inmates didn't even know how to feel or how to identify or label their feelings. This was one of the particular exercises that we would do in group settings - how to identify and label feelings. For example, there's the feeling of anger, but what about all the different types of emotions that can fall under the realm of anger? It could be frustration, irritability, or rage. There are so many expressions and forms of "anger," but they were all labeled as anger.

The same goes for happiness. The inmates would be able to identify happy, sad, and angry, and this was about it, but not dig any deeper into other forms of happiness, such as excitement, joy, feeling content, etc.

I would do an exercise with them and ask them to identify other feelings that fall under the umbrella terms of happiness, sadness, and anger. This is when they would learn about other "happiness" emotions, like the ones listed above.

The beauty of these emotions is that there are so many of them, and emotions are so complex, but the thing about being human and experiencing this human condition is to experience all these emotions and allow them to exist. This also includes the emotions that don't feel good.

One thing I want to emphasize, and I emphasize this a lot in my sessions also, is that whatever it is that you're feeling, it's okay to feel that way. I don't care what it is, whether it's anger, rage, jealousy, excitement, sadness, or disgust. No matter what the emotion is, whatever it is that you're feeling, by default, that feeling is valid for the very reason that you're feeling it.

Now, what we do with that emotion is a whole different thing, and that's also a different chapter, so I'm not going to spend too much time on that here. However, one of the things that I think is important to remember, especially as a counselor and from the things that I've experienced through all my years working with many, many people, is that going through the bad stuff is okay.

It's okay to feel it and allow those feelings that feel bad to exist. It's okay to experience them. There's no need to be perfect today. There's no need for everything to be exactly right today. Of course, it's good to strive for that, and it's always good to have goals and to want to improve and, at the same time, to feel okay with where you're at right now.

We get into this black-and-white thinking, this either/or thinking. For example, we have a tendency to think that if we don't do this thing right, then we fail, instead of acknowledging that maybe we didn't accomplish this thing, but at the same time, we're also a success, and we'll try harder next time.

We tend to place too much emphasis on this outcome and this goal without recognizing that, at the same time, we're still living today. Every single experience is still part of being human, not the intended goal or outcome. I cannot emphasize this enough because this alone causes a lot of conflicting emotions in people.

Failure is part of the human condition, the human experience. We set out to accomplish a goal, whatever that goal might be, and we give in to something, and we don't quite meet the goal; well, guess what? That's part of the human experience!

> **Struggling doesn't mean you're broken; it means you're human.**

Trying again and again to improve is important, but at the same time, it's also essential to recognize that what we experience daily is also good, failures included.

If you want to enjoy that greasy burger, that's part of the human experience! Instead of making yourself feel guilty about it, why not enjoy it and savor it instead? You're then allowing yourself to feel what you're feeling instead of feeling bad for what you're feeling.

Another thing that we often do is emphasize that we shouldn't feel a certain way. When I talk about the negative stuff being okay, what I mean is that there's a place for it to exist. It's about recognizing that it's a part of your existence and accepting that into your life as part of your experience. This is not the same as saying that whatever happened is okay because, a lot of times, things happen that are simply not okay. That's not what I'm talking about here. What I'm saying is that the existence of emotions and the fact that the feeling is present is okay.

Something happened to cause you to feel emotions that don't feel good. The thing that happened might not necessarily be okay, but how you feel about it, that feeling is okay.

> **Even your tears are part of a beautiful human moment.**

I believe it's important to recognize that we often tell ourselves we shouldn't feel a certain way or that our feelings are bad. We judge ourselves for certain things. But I'm here to tell you no. Whatever you're feeling, it's okay.

Don't feel guilty about how you feel! You feel how you feel! Now, what you do with those feelings is a whole different matter because it's only ever in our behaviors and our actions that we experience consequences. We can feel whatever we feel and think whatever we want to think; it's always only the behaviors that cause the consequences.

Essentially, your feelings are always valid, and feeling them is a part of being human. You're having a human experience, and that's okay.

When we experience emotional pain, one of our first responses is that we don't want to feel this way, and we want to experience something different. We can distract ourselves from our emotional pain, or we can repress and stuff our emotions and try to avoid them. We can find ways not to deal with our emotional pain by not thinking about it and by putting our minds somewhere else. Maybe we even distract ourselves with very unhealthy habits. But one thing that we don't do is see the existing emotion as a guide, and that it's telling us something.

Say, for example, I'm in physical pain, and I experience a little pain in my side. Then, I'll probably acknowledge that pain and simply start by identifying that my stomach hurts. I might even tell myself that I probably pulled a muscle or something like that, and tell myself that I'll be fine, whatever. Then, I go about my day not thinking too much about it. Then, the next day, I feel the pain again, and maybe I'll tell myself, wow, I guess I worked out harder than I thought, or still downplay this pain. Then I wake up the next day, and my side still hurts, maybe a little worse than the day before. But then I also acknowledge that if this was muscle pain, the pain should be less today. Then, the next day, it hurts a little more.

Now, if this pain persists, I know that I'm not supposed to feel this way, and I know it's not normal for me to feel this pain consistently. If it's persistent and I have no idea what it is, then there's a very good chance that I'm getting this checked out because the pain is my body's way of telling me that there's something wrong.

Emotions work the same way. If you wake up angry every single day, instead of suppressing your anger, distracting yourself from your anger through maybe unhealthy habits, going about your day in an angry mood all day, or being angry at everyone you see, listen to the message that your anger is telling you. Like pain in the body, it's a warning sign telling you there's something wrong.

If you're waking up every single day with some kind of emotion that doesn't feel good, then that's your emotional system telling you there's something wrong. Maybe something in your life needs to change, or you need to work through something to feel better.

With this in mind, it's also important to keep in mind the short-term versus the long-term. When I talk about the bad stuff being okay, that all these emotions that don't feel good are part of the human condition, I'm also talking about initial reactions and initial emotions.

If someone betrays you, you're going to feel incredibly hurt and angry about that. You have every right to feel this way! Or if someone says something, and you feel offended and hurt, then that feeling is valid. Or if you're looking forward to something and you're excited about it, that feeling is valid, as well. But when a negative feeling persists, then it's no longer a response to a particular situation, and you may feel stuck in this negative emotion. For example, with grief, if you lose someone that you love and you miss them so much, and you go through the grief process, it's going to mimic all the symptoms of depression, and you're going to feel it.

When you wake up, you might feel lost. You might have low energy, no appetite, and sleep disruption. Your mood might be low, and you're irritable. These symptoms mimic the same symptoms as depression, but it's not depression. You're responding to a loss, and therefore, these feelings are a response to something. Sometimes, this can take a while to get through, and at the same time, it's temporary.

Depression, on the other hand, is not particularly an immediate response to a particular situation. Sometimes, it can start as a response to something, but when it persists and you're waking up every single day feeling unhappy, that is your emotional system telling you there's something wrong.

Like physical pain you might experience, you're getting a signal that something needs to be addressed, so instead of going through your day every day with low moods, it's an opportunity to explore what can change in your life and how you can address these feelings, so you can start feeling better.

Sometimes, I get feedback from people wondering if it would be easier not to feel anything at all. They think that life would be simpler if they didn't have to feel anything; then they wouldn't feel hurt and would never feel pain, betrayal, loss, or loneliness. It might sound good to never feel those things anymore, and sometimes it might sound appealing; however, if you never feel, then you're also never going to experience the emotions that feel good, such as joy or happiness.

If you think back to a beautiful day that you've had, maybe when you've connected with someone close to you and everything about that day was great, and you felt such joy in that day because everything was going right, well, if you never felt, then the joy of this day wouldn't happen either.

We end up needing our emotions because they are very much our guide in life. Sometimes, it might feel easier not to feel anything, but emotions can be very telling, too. Like physical pain, we need pain because we need a warning system that helps us keep our bodies in check. For instance, if I conclude that physical pain sucks and I hate it, and nothing about physical pain is good, I may then wish that I never experienced pain at all. Suddenly, a genie comes along and grants me my wish of never experiencing physical pain ever again.

Now I go about my day, and I feel great! I can do all these amazing things because I'm not feeling pain, and then I step on a rusty nail. Well, I don't feel it, and I don't know that I stepped on a rusty nail because I don't feel pain, and when do I ever look at the bottom of my feet? As time goes on, my foot is going to get infected, and it's going to get worse, and eventually, it's going to result in a horrible outcome. I needed that pain to tell me that there was something wrong so that I could take care of it and heal myself.

The same goes for our emotions. Even though we experience joy and a lot of the positive things, we also need the negatives because they're a guide.

There's a two-fold thing to this. The first part, which is the big emphasis that I'm making, is that there's room for these emotions that don't feel good. There's a place to accept the whole realm of emotions, no matter what those emotions are. There's no pressure to have to feel something different. I believe this is so important because your feelings are valid, and like I've said before, the feelings that you're feeling are part of the human experience, so accept those experiences in your life.

I challenge you, next time you're feeling hurt, upset, or facing a tough moment, to remind yourself that you are having a beautiful experience. Like when you're crying or when you're upset, and there's something that's going on in your life, whether it's loss or hurt or disappointment, I want you to challenge yourself that while you're feeling hurt, and as you're in the middle of all of those emotions, to remind yourself that you're having a beautiful human experience. The intensity of the emotions that you're feeling right in that moment is part of this beautiful human experience that you're living, and at the same time, knowing that whatever you're feeling in any given moment, you won't feel that way forever.

The second part of this two-fold concept is to use your emotions as a guide to tell you what it is that you're feeling, so that you can continue to work on improving things. Even though there's a place for sadness, and this feeling is valid, it's important not to get stuck in this feeling with no resolve. When you identify that your emotions don't feel good every day and you're not responding to anything, use that emotion as a warning sign, as a big blinking neon sign telling you something's wrong, and then work on addressing this and moving to change how you feel.

If you felt pain under your foot because you stepped on a rusty nail, you would never ignore that pain or tell yourself that this sharp pain under your foot is probably nothing! You wouldn't ignore it and put some anesthetic on it or take painkillers and hope it goes away without knowing what's going on! It sounds absurd to think we would do that with physical pain, but we do exactly that when it comes to emotional pain.

Therefore, I challenge you to live and experience your emotions without shame and judgment because it's part of your precious human experience.

4
REVIEWING GOALS

In this chapter, I'd like to talk about being a little more flexible in our lives because, too often, we can be too rigid, especially in our thinking. This concept was highlighted through an experience with one of my clients, but I found this theme recurring with other clients as well. I also want to talk about the idea that sometimes our needs and our wants change, but we don't necessarily realize this. So we hold on to an idea and become fixated on something, and then it becomes quite rigid in our minds.

Sometimes, we hold on to ideas because they made us happy in the past, but that doesn't mean that this is still relevant. But because it made us happy, or it fulfilled a need in the past, we hold on to it, thinking the same thing is going to make us happy again in the future. Circumstances change, and whatever it was that met our needs in the past might not work the same way in the future.

There's more than one way to get where you want to go, if you're willing to look around.

The other idea that goes along with this is that sometimes, the path to get to the same goal changes. When we have an idea about our goals or in what direction we are headed to achieve a certain outcome, we also may have an idea of what we need to do to get there. This may have worked in the past, but that doesn't mean that this same path is what we need in the present. We might need to take a step back and review what works for us and what doesn't. We might need to be more open to something different.

The way I identified this concept was while working with a client who was struggling with a sense of losing her connection to spirituality. She used to be part of a spiritual community, and her beliefs used to be a very big part of who she was. She used to feel very secure in her beliefs and spirituality; she felt very safe and connected in it. She felt that spirituality overall was a very active part of her life and even a part of her identity.

This significant part of her life also used to make her feel connected to the bigger picture. She felt like her life had meaning and purpose, but over time, she felt like her belief was slowly fading away. When she came into my office, part of what she wanted to talk about was how to get that spiritual connection back.

In therapy, we explored this, and we explored a lot of the typical things that fall in the realm of being connected spiritually. We explored the idea of meditating regularly, but this didn't work for her and felt more like a chore than anything else. She had difficulty getting into meditation practice and committing the time for this. For her, this meditation practice didn't feel like a spiritual thing or something that made her feel connected.

We talked about some other things she could explore, like journaling or writing about her emotions, thoughts, and spiritual beliefs, but whereas this was something that normally could help a lot of people, for her, this felt like a chore. She felt it was something she had to do, and then it felt forced.

Then we explored other avenues that could make her feel more spiritually connected. One of the things that came up was gardening. She loved gardening, and we talked about connecting in this way, as gardening was also very much a hands-on experience. Gardening involves getting your hands dirty when you're potting and planting, and this could help her feel more connected to nature. The other spiritual aspect of gardening that we discussed was being able to see things grow as a direct result of the care she provided to the garden. In this aspect, gardening could be very nurturing.

Even though she enjoyed gardening, she didn't feel that this was something that necessarily connected her to something spiritual. So, as we explored this concept further, one thing that came up was that she also didn't feel that her job had purpose and meaning, and she didn't feel fulfilled in that way either. When she didn't feel spiritually connected anymore, she also recognized that the job she was in, which was a significant chunk of her waking life, was not very meaningful or fulfilling to her. She started to lose her excitement in her job because it was something that wasn't providing her any satisfaction.

As we continued to explore this realm of her life, one thing she identified was that in the past, when she felt deeply connected, it was partly due to the network she was involved with. She lived in a house with others who were connected to the spiritual network, and they all got together regularly, so she was very much an active part of this community.

That was the part that she identified as lacking in her life, so she was making the association between feeling spiritually connected, but also very much socially connected.

This insight allowed us to explore whether part of her spiritual connection was feeling like a part of her social connection was missing. However, she did not feel connected with other people, regardless of whether spirituality played a role in this or not. She recognized that her job was also isolated and didn't allow her to make meaningful connections with others.

She explored this new avenue of connecting with friends more and the possibility of rebuilding connections or making new connections so that she could feel more connected in some way, a connection that she had attributed to being a spiritual connection, but was a connection in general.

This worked to some degree. She did start to feel a little more connected to others, and that her life had a bit more meaning. She started to feel a greater fulfillment in life, but then another thing she started to explore was some other career opportunities that allowed for a greater sense of meaning and purpose in her job.

We explored the idea of building meaning and purpose through her career, especially as one's job is a significant part of one's life, and she identified that she felt her current job did not give her a sense of purpose or contribution. She identified that she'd always had a passion for teaching and that she had always wanted to be in a position of teaching younger children, making an impact on their lives, connecting with young students, and helping them learn.

She ended up pursuing this route and got a teaching degree that allowed her to work in the school system. She put her notice in at her job, and now her career is more in the realm of what she had in mind with spiritual connection, because her new career is going to have purpose and meaning. Even if there are difficult days in her new job, she also knows that she's making a difference and is impacting the lives of young children.

The key points from this journey are that she had lost a spiritual connection she once had and wanted to regain it. For her, it was very much the idea of something spiritual, feeling a greater sense of meaning, but specifically spiritually. So, this is the first thing we began to explore.

However, on further exploration, it wasn't necessarily a spiritual connection; it was simply a connection and being an active part of something meaningful. We identified that one of the big aspects of her life, when she did feel spiritually connected, was that she was very much socially connected because her spiritual network was very much connected through them getting together, and she was an active participant in this.

The other piece of this was that in her past, she felt that her life had a purpose. She felt fulfilled, and there was meaning because she was aligned with a higher purpose, a higher presence. But when we explored the different avenues where she could have this same experience, she realized it didn't have to be through spiritual means. This is how she found out that she could create exactly that same feeling of fulfillment, but through her job instead, and this is the path that she took.

One thing I want to point out in writing about this is that sometimes we desire something simply because it worked for us in the past. However, when we explore it further, maybe it's not exactly what we need today. Maybe those needs have changed.

Sometimes, we have an idea or plan in our mind about what we need, and we hold on to it. But when we begin to pursue the path that we think we need, it doesn't feel the same and doesn't work out as expected. That's because the result might be the same, but the path to get there is different.

For instance, with my client, she wanted connection and fulfillment, and this was the result. However, in the past, her spiritual network was her path toward this, but in the present, it had changed, and she was able to reach the same results through a very different path - her career.

I believe that there are many examples of how this manifests in our lives. For example, when you're exploring different career paths, you might have an idea of what you want to pursue but not realize that there may be many other avenues that lead to the same thing. When you're very set on a path and how you're going to accomplish something, you might be limiting your other options as well.

What I want to share from this idea is to encourage you to explore whether the path toward your end goal is rigid or whether there are other ways you can reach your same goal. Is there room for flexibility, or is there room for finding that same outcome in different ways?

Success isn't always about changing direction. Sometimes, it's about changing definition.

For example, if someone comes to me stating they want to be happier and they want to experience more happiness and joy in their life, maybe they are experiencing depression or a sense of loneliness, or a lack of fulfillment. Sometimes, they may identify a rigid end goal that will cause happiness, e.g., they tell themselves that they will be happy when they meet a significant other, or they will be happy when debt is paid off, or when they get their super-toned abs. However, they might not consider that there are so many ways to create a greater sense of happiness, and this is not necessarily through only one means.

For example, an individual who thinks they will only be happy once they meet a significant other may come to realize that they are lonely and isolated, and therefore create a connection with anyone and get involved in the community somehow, not necessarily through a partner per se, and this reframe may increase feelings of happiness.

The individual who feels that happiness will come from wealth may come to realize that life's worth is valued by so much more than material gains, and through reassessing how they place worth and value in their life, come to feel much richer, even with debts in place.

You might even find that you're rigid with health goals, believing that only a strict diet or some strict exercise routine will get you there when, in fact, any type of improved health practices will help you move toward greater health.

In essence, the gist is that you must first identify what your goal is because, as we have seen in this chapter, your identified goal may not necessarily be what you're looking for. When you identify what it is you truly want versus what you think you want and allow yourself to be more flexible with the path to your goal, you open up greater opportunities to succeed toward your intended outcome.

5

CAN YOU FIND YOURSELF?

One common theme that comes back a lot in counseling, or maybe even in a general existential or philosophical way, is people wanting to find out who they are. I get clients in my office telling me they want to find out who they are or if a behavior is theirs. I've thought about this question or concept a lot, and I struggle with it.

The reason why I struggle so much with it is how do you know whether you've found yourself? What does that even mean? I've always had trouble figuring out what finding out who you are even means because I think I struggle with identifying the result, like what lets you know that you have found yourself? At what point can you truly answer this?

You're not a riddle to be solved;
you're a person in motion.

What is it about who you are that tells you who you are? Is "who you are" defined by your actions? I feel like exploring this topic a little further because, to tell you the truth, I don't even know if there's such a thing as finding who you are!

I believe that maybe who you are is all about you at the moment, and who you are creating, but also may be an accumulation of your actions from the past. One of the general concepts of who we are is whether we are good or bad. And how do you define that? For example, what makes a person good or bad? I would suggest that what makes a person good or bad is an accumulation of their actions. If a person does a lot of bad things, does that make them a bad person? I think it may be reasonable to argue that yes, this is quite likely. Likewise, if someone does a lot of good things, are they then a good person?

It seems like the logical answer to this would be that your actions then define who you are. One of the things that I delve into further in another chapter is the triangle of thoughts, feelings, and behaviors. These are three different things, so you have thoughts, which are all the things you think about, your beliefs, and the running dialogue in your head. Then there are feelings, your emotions, and how you feel about situations. But then you have your actions, which are the things you do, and it's only ever your actions that have any consequences. You can think whatever you want to think, and you can feel whatever you're feeling, but the only thing that will cause consequences in yourself and other people is what you do, i.e., your behaviors and your actions.

I believe that the concept of who you are could be defined by looking at your actions, the things you do, the way you would normally choose to respond in a situation, and does that ultimately define who you are?

For example, if you're wondering whether you are a good person or a bad person, then maybe it's about looking at your actions and figuring out if you generally do good or bad things. Do you generally hurt people or help people? Do you generally judge and criticize others or accept others?

Exploring this even further, we can even question whether defining something as good or bad is subjective. Nevertheless, maybe a good place to start in exploring who we are is to begin by looking at your actions and your reactions to different things.

Another thing to elaborate on is how you define that. How do you define who you are? I am... well; I am a daughter, a sister, a mental health counselor, a harpist, an athlete, etc. However, do these concepts define who I am? These are aspects of myself, and there are probably thousands of ways I can define myself... I'm a female with large hands and feet, average height, blonde, and on and on and on.

So then, what are the factors that ultimately define who we are? If we're discussing finding out who we are, then we also have to figure out what it is that defines us. And who can say what that is? We all define ourselves in different ways. Some people define themselves in a way that says, "My name is such-and-such, and I am such-and-such." Some people define themselves by their career, so that becomes who they are. My name is Louise, and I'm a mental health counselor. Okay, that's who I am, but I'm a mental health counselor, and I'm also a thousand other things, too.

The definition of who I am includes being a mental health counselor, but is not limited to this. To even discuss finding out who we are, it becomes such a broad subject, and can we even begin to understand it, or can we even begin to explore it?

Maybe the biggest struggle I have with finding who we are is how we will know when we've found it? In the end, aren't we us, right now in this moment? Who am I? I'm me, right now, right here. That's all there is to it! Right? How else can I define myself? How else can I truly know who I am? Am I a loving person? Well, I don't need to explore this because I can ask myself this based on my actions. Am I respectable? Well, have I done respectable things? Am I an athlete? Well, do I do athletic things? I think maybe the reason I struggle with finding who you are is because, to me, there's nothing to look for! There's nothing to find. I don't ever think that there's this hidden aspect of ourselves that we didn't know before that will suddenly be revealed to us when we begin searching for who we are. I don't think something will be revealed that makes us go, "Oh! This is who I am!"

I think that maybe the biggest definition or maybe an aspect of the definition of who we are is who we are today and an accumulation of everything that we've done up to the present moment.

There are a few other things I'd like to elaborate on. One of the things I've noticed is that we often define who we are by our differences. The thing that makes us stand out from the crowd is quite often the thing that we define ourselves through. This could also be a minority, a skill set, or a talent. For example, I am Sam, and I am gay, or I am Louise, and I am Dutch and northern English.

We often seem to find ourselves through our minorities, and through the traits and skills that make us stand out. Then, you can get into a discussion about identity because that is something that is inherently very important to us.

So maybe another aspect of finding who we are is about making sense of our beliefs, our preferences, our tastes, and the things that appeal to us. Maybe a part of who we are comes from our identity. For example, one big way that people identify themselves is through their ancestry. People feel good about knowing who they are based on their ancestry.

I know a lot of individuals who are in America; they've lived in America their whole life, but they identify as a certain nationality because of their ancestry, e.g., I'm Italian! They've never been to Italy, they don't speak any Italian words, they don't engage in Italian customs or celebrate Italian holidays, and their ancestors have been in America for generations, but because ultimately their ancestry goes back into Italy, they identify as Italian, even when they have no personal experience of anything Italian.

However, something like this can almost define a person because it becomes a part of their identity and, thereby, also a part of finding who they are.

**Who you are is not a single fact.
It's an evolving story.**

I think maybe another aspect of making sense of who you are through your ancestry is because it helps us make sense of our likes and dislikes, e.g., someone might say that they love the cold and gloomy rainy weather because they're Scottish or English, or they love a certain food that is native to their ancestry.

It seems like people, in general, need some kind of identity, and this may also be one of the reasons why the concept of finding who you are is a popular concept, even though it doesn't make any sense.

So, maybe one aspect of figuring out who you are is figuring out your identity. And finding out your identity can be done in different ways. I believe through my experience that your identity is something that you define yourself. It becomes a very subjective definition.

For example, for individuals in the LGBTQ+ realm, a lot of people's identity falls in this realm, and this becomes the biggest defining factor in how they identify themselves. Even though there are a thousand things, the ultimate defining factor is the LGBTQ+ realm because this is, at that moment, the most significant and prevalent, or important.

Maybe, then, the concept of finding who you are is a very subjective thing. When we ponder the question of what makes you who you are, how do you know that this defining feature makes you who you are, or why is it that particular defining factor? What do I use to define myself, and is it different from what you use to define me?

Maybe the things that I use to define me are very different from the factors that someone else uses to define them, so this becomes very subjective. Someone who is heterosexual might never place the heterosexual identity as a defining characteristic of who they are, but a gay individual may be a lot quicker to define who they are as gay because this is a minority, and therefore, something that makes them stand out from the norm.

Another individual may define who they are based on nationality or through their ancestry, and yet others might define who they are through their education, achievements or profession.

This is why I believe people will often define themselves through their differences. If I introduce myself as my name is Louise and I am a human, well, so is everyone else. Or I am Louise, and I am female, and even though this is part of my identity, half of the world's population is also female.

We use characteristics that set us apart from the majority, e.g., my name is Louise, and I am Dutch. Most people are not from the Netherlands, so having a Dutch identity more clearly defines who I am, as it makes me stand out from the majority. By saying "I'm Dutch," I could also be implying that I like certain things and don't like certain things, based on the typical Dutch personality.

This might also give me a sense of who I am because then I also get a better sense of my preferences, my likes and dislikes, and the things that I lean toward. And we find comfort in being able to identify a certain way.

Maybe part of the comfort comes from the fact that by establishing a certain identity, we can better predict ourselves or better make sense of ourselves.

I find that exploring the concept of who we are is about going back to who we are at any given moment. It involves three elements, i.e., the past, the present, and the future, because when you talk about finding who you are, ultimately, you're looking at yourself in the present. There's only you right now. Who you are is who you are right now. You are not who you were ten years ago, and you're not who you were as a child. We all learn and grow and change. Our beliefs and values are constantly changing based on new information and learning, so our outlooks and perspectives, our likes and dislikes, and everything that contributes to the accumulation of who we are is always changing. Our goals change, the things that we fight for change, and our roles in society change, so who we are is forever changing.

Then, it becomes more about who we are at any given moment in time. So now we're working with the present because if you want to find who you are, then you have to look at who you are right now. Only you, right now, exist.

However, the past comes into play because who you are right now is an accumulation of your experiences. It's all those past things that make you who you are, like wondering if you're a good person or a bad person. When we look at our past actions, we can better determine who we are in the present. This even applies to the ways we define ourselves, e.g., if I want to know if I'm a mental health counselor, do my past actions of education and professional experience determine that I am a mental health counselor today? Whether I can call myself an athlete is in part determined by my experiences of having done athletic things. If I want to know if I'm loved, I can determine this by determining whether people around me have shown me love.

So identifying and finding who you are acknowledges that only you exist in the present, and at the same time, you in this present moment are an accumulation of your past. But it also involves the future, and this is when I think about one of my favorite quotes, by Henry David Thoreau: "Life is not about finding yourself, it's about creating yourself." And this resonates a lot more.

Finding who you are - is there such a thing? Does it even exist? How will you know? What will change? What will be different? How do you define such a thing? Isn't finding who we are, then, a lifelong process with no result? We're forever changing, so who we are is very fluid. Is it then based on every single decision we make at every moment in time? Am I going to be nice to this individual right now, at this moment, or not? All these momentary decisions are constantly shaping who we are.

Therefore, finding who you are is not a fixed or static thing, and maybe this is why the answer to this question is so elusive. Maybe this is also why we use identity, such as ancestry, because those things are fixed and will never change. However, characteristics are constantly changing.

I resonate with Thoreau's quote about life not being about finding yourself but about creating yourself, and that right there is a beautiful thing. When you ask about wanting to find out who you are, maybe instead of asking yourself who you are, the better question is, who do you want to be?

When you begin to ask yourself who you want to be instead of who you are, then you're looking at your ideal self and figuring out who that person is. Then, through your choices, you begin to create that. If you create drama and conflict everywhere, and you want to be a kinder person, you can create that. You can create that by the choices you make in every moment! If you want to be loved, then you can begin to create that by changing the way you interact with individuals and thereby influencing the response. If you want to be a kind and giving person, but you know that in the present you're not, then you can become this kind and loving person by beginning to do kind and loving things.

Who we are is always fluid and changing, and who we are in the present is a result of our past actions, so even though now you might not be this kind and loving individual, you can become this kind and loving person by engaging in kind and loving acts, and then your past actions of kindness and love will establish you as a kind and loving person. You've now created this in yourself by the choices you've made.

Finding who you are is who you are today, but that's always subject to change because you can now create who you are! I think Thoreau got it spot on when he says that life isn't about finding yourself; it's about creating yourself, and I think this is a much more relevant question.

When I have clients come into my office, and they want to find out who they are, this is usually the discussion that I have with them. I ask my clients what they are looking for when they're trying to figure out who they are, and usually what they're trying to do is to figure out if they are a certain way, but in the end, they can create whoever they want to be by changing their choices at the moment.

6

CHANGING BOUNDARIES

Let's explore the topic of boundaries and where boundaries ultimately come from. On exploring this concept further, questions arise about where boundaries come from and how we can change boundaries. Sometimes, it feels like changing boundaries can be extremely difficult, an observation I have made countless times in my practice. Sometimes, we know that we should say no more often or that we need to better protect ourselves and not allow certain people in our lives, but at the same time, it seems incredibly difficult to put this into practice.

It's all good and well to educate someone and tell them how letting people walk all over you is unhealthy, even telling them that they need to learn to say no more, but most likely, they know this already on a logical and cognitive level but still have difficulty connecting with this on an emotional level.

I started thinking about how we can change this on a level that works. How can we see an individual who is very confident in their ability to say no and who has very healthy boundaries, and then someone else who doesn't? Both individuals know what's healthy for them and what isn't, but why does the individual who is very capable of setting healthy boundaries do this more easily? What is different about this individual from someone who struggles with boundaries?

I started to explore where boundaries come from, and what I identified is that boundaries come from your values. The values you have in your life will often help with your boundaries, so whatever value you place or what your values are, that helps determine how you place your boundaries.

If you take this another step further, we can ask where our values come from. In my exploration, values come from our outlook on the world, i.e., the way we form our perspective on the world around us. In turn, our outlook on the world comes from our beliefs about the world, i.e., how we make sense of the world based on our experiences and observations, etc.

Boundaries teach others how to treat us.

Learning how we make sense of the world is a series of associations. We learn because we piece things together, and this gives us a sense of how things will be in the future. For example, if I put my hand on the stove and burn it, I'll associate the stove with heat and know to be more careful - probably not doing it again!

So, our experiences and observations help form our beliefs about the world, and this, in turn, determines our outlook. We then form our values based on this outlook, and this leads to how we place our boundaries.

Say, for example, that part of my life experience is that I was bitten by a dog. Then, this becomes part of my history, and I learn from this. I subconsciously make associations, and this life experience creates a belief, maybe that dogs are bad, or dogs are dangerous, or dogs can hurt you. With that belief system, I'm now making sense of something, and then I form an outlook, a perspective of the world that says I need to be careful around dogs because dogs can bite, dogs can hurt, and that doesn't feel good.

So my outlook on the world includes that dogs are dangerous or that dogs can be harmful. That outlook has now become part of my value system. When I create a value system, and part of this value system includes that dogs are not okay, and I want to protect myself from getting hurt, then part of my boundaries is going to be that I'm going to be careful around dogs, and I'm not going to get close to dogs. You might even develop a weariness of some dogs over others, e.g., dogs who are similar to the dog that bit you.

Of course, this is a loose and simplified example of where boundaries come from, but this manifests in so many ways. Here is another example. Say that someone grew up in a poor household in a dysfunctional setting. Maybe the parents didn't care about them, and so this individual grows up with the message about themselves that they're not important. Maybe at one point, they tried hard in school, and they were successful in school and were very excited about telling their parents about a particular achievement, but when they did, the parents didn't show any enthusiasm, reinforcing the message that they don't matter and they're not important.

So, now, this child, in a very subconscious way, begins to develop this belief system about themselves. I don't matter. I don't matter to my parents, and I don't matter in this world.

When I say that this becomes part of their belief system, I don't mean that they think this on a conscious level. They're not making a conscious decision by going okay, and I'm now making this decision to have this belief about the world. No, this happens on a very internal, subconscious level. They start to slowly feel it, and whenever something happens that reinforces this message, the feelings and beliefs become stronger.

When someone starts forming a subconscious belief about themselves that they don't matter, then when something happens to affirm that belief, it strengthens that conviction.

So the negative belief system of "I don't matter" could even turn into "I'm not lovable," "not deserving of love," or "not worthy." Now, because of these belief systems, part of their outlook on the world turns into the belief that nobody cares about them. They begin to believe that they don't matter to people, and because of this belief system, they see this reinforced in their everyday lives.

Now, their outlook begins to shape their value system, which becomes compromised because they start with the belief that they don't matter to others, and this evolves into a feeling of low self-worth.

Now that this is the value that they've learned to place on themselves, based on their experience, this now forms a belief that shapes their perspective of the world around them.

This belief system about themselves and the world around them is reflected back in their value system. If someone has a low value about themselves, this also means that this individual will likely allow a lot more different types of individuals in their lives because they don't feel they are worthy of better and healthier individuals.

Quite often, these types of individuals may attract abusive partners, psychologically and verbally, as well as physically. They are more likely to allow people who treat them negatively to take advantage of their poor boundaries because they are allowing all sorts of different things into their lives; they don't feel they deserve better.

In order to help someone change these kinds of boundaries, it's often frustrating to tell them that they shouldn't let people treat them in this way or let people walk all over them. As I mentioned earlier, they know this logically but are still not able to say no or set healthier boundaries because even though they know that some people in their lives are not healthy, what hasn't changed is part of their value system.

> **The boundary problem isn't about saying no.**
> **It's about believing you're allowed to.**

The value system is the thing that needs to change, i.e., the change needs to go deeper than on a cognitive level. If you want to help others change their boundaries, or if you want to change your own and improve the way you take care of yourself, you have to go deeper.

This is where you can start to explore and go back through the cycle. For example, you can start to explore how boundaries come from values. You can explore your values. This is when you start to identify that you have low self-worth or have a low value about yourself, and you can start to explore where this comes from and why this is present in your life, and why this value is in place in your life.

Part of the reason this value is in place in different individuals is because of their outlook that nobody cares about them or that they don't matter. They may have the outlook that people suck or that people only look out for themselves and take advantage of others, and when people are nice to them, it's because they want something. Ironically, this outlook will allow them to see more of this in the life around them because their focus is attuned to identifying this, like you see the make and model of your car everywhere right after you bought yours.

After exploring and identifying the outlook, you can ask yourself, well, where does this outlook, this perspective, come from? It is now part of that individual's belief system, so what made them create these belief systems about the world around them? Why do some people create a belief system that people are inherently good, and others create a belief system that people are inherently bad? Well, it usually comes from their lived experiences.

This can also lead to a deeper exploration, e.g., exploring experiences from childhood that contributed to these belief systems. Maybe an individual identifies that their parents never cared about them, and they felt like they didn't matter. Or they may remember how they did a lot of great things in school and worked hard, but nobody acknowledged this, adding to this feeling of not mattering.

By going back through lived experiences, you can begin to explore where those different beliefs came from, and in my experience as a therapist, I can say that most of these beliefs formed very early on, like a snowball getting bigger and stronger over time. It's how we make sense of the world, so when we form a belief about something and then something happens that reinforces our already existing beliefs, it's like our subconscious says, "See, I knew I was right," and this belief becomes stronger.

We learn through association or conditioning, so if we believe that nobody loves us, then we must be unlovable. And, like I mentioned before, this isn't a conscious thought or decision. It's not like we think logically and rationally because I feel like nobody loves me, therefore, I must be unlovable. No. These things happen in the deep recesses of our subconscious and start to grow and mold over time. But now, with this knowledge, you can go back and explore the origins of these beliefs.

By exploring the childhood pattern (how we begin to make sense of the world and the associations formed in our earlier years), we start to identify how we formed our beliefs about the world.

Our beliefs about the world around us are how we started to form our perspective of the world. This perspective is about how we make sense of the world. The basic concept is that if I do A and then do B, it leads to C. If I don't do A or B, then C isn't going to happen, so this is what I need to do.

> **Every belief you've absorbed can be questioned and rewritten.**

Life is all about learning. It's all conditioning and making associations, so in therapy, when I explore someone's experiences and how they got to certain beliefs, then I can also understand how they got to the different beliefs about themselves and the outlook they have about the world around them in the present. That outlook ultimately creates their values.

When you start challenging someone's life experiences and help them understand that maybe their parents didn't give them the time of day and that in their young brain, they associated this with their parents not loving them, and therefore they must be unlovable, now we can challenge that and question that.

Does feeling unloved by your parents make you unlovable? Of course not! Now, we can work toward changing some of those ultimate belief systems and assumptions we've made from where they started. And when you start changing those internal ingrained beliefs, that is when you begin changing this whole cycle.

When I work with a client with the core internal belief that they aren't lovable, toward the belief that they are lovable, they can begin to change the way they see the past. For example, maybe they realize that their parents do love them, but they had a very difficult time showing love, perhaps through their own childhood experiences. But this doesn't mean they are unlovable. Therefore, if they are lovable, then that means they are worthy of love, and this means they are deserving of love, and this then changes the value they hold toward themselves.

Of course, this process doesn't happen overnight. It won't be an instant insight in one moment in time, but rather through repeated affirmations and being able to change one's perspective of how they experienced their earlier years. What happened is years and years of conditioning that caused this individual to get to this moment in time, like I wrote in my previous chapter about creating neural pathways through repetition, and so through continued repetition of positive reframes, an individual can slowly work on changing those internal negative belief systems.

For example, if you stand in front of a mirror feeling unworthy of love, or if your experiences have shown that people don't care about you or love you, saying "I'm lovable" to the reflection may feel like a comical farce. Some people are even unable to say the words out loud because they feel like they are completely lying to themselves! But this is also exactly where the work starts.

What you're doing through continued repetition of new thoughts and ideas is you're changing some of the belief systems in those neural pathways. So, even though it might feel like you're telling yourself the biggest lie initially, you can slowly begin to change some of those beliefs over time.

The message of not being lovable or whatever negative belief system is present in your subconscious didn't happen in one sitting, either. It's highly unlikely that you had a healthy, solid upbringing, and then you came home with a good grade, and your parents were too busy to notice, and at that moment in time, your subconscious believed you were no longer lovable. It doesn't happen like that. At that time, you might be incredibly disappointed because your parents were too busy to notice you, but when you receive other messages of being loved, then this disappointment doesn't have as much significance. The damage comes from the repetition of the message and the repeated confirmation of a belief system that is reaffirmed over and over through other experiences. When you receive repeated messages of not being loved or that you don't matter, then you start to see that more and more in your life, and this is what creates the negative core belief systems.

If you have an internal belief of not feeling loved, then you're not going to change this overnight by deciding that you are lovable. You may know this cognitively, but your feelings won't line up immediately because the feelings come from the subconscious and run a lot deeper. You don't immediately start believing something in the subconscious, in your core, because you make a conscious choice to believe something new. You have to do this through repetition, over and over and over, because only through repetition will you begin to see new life experiences that affirm your new belief system, and this is when your negative belief system will slowly morph into a more positive outlook.

As I mentioned, at first, this might feel like the biggest joke, but over time, you may start believing aspects of it, and then a life event may happen that shows that someone does care about you. This will affirm your new belief system and thereby strengthen it; that's how you start changing the cycle.

The cycle is that your boundaries stem from your values, your values come from your outlook on the world, your outlook stems from your beliefs, and your beliefs come from your life experiences. So when you look at your life experiences, and then you start challenging the beliefs you've created around those experiences, you change the story you've told yourself about your life experiences.

When you say, "My parents didn't show me love, and therefore, I'm not lovable and I don't matter," now we start challenging that belief system. You do matter; you are lovable, and just because your parents didn't show it, doesn't mean that it's true. You might not have received much love from your parents, but at the same time, you can receive love from other people.

Now you can start challenging some of those belief systems, and what happens is that through time, a person starts believing that they do matter, that they can be loved, and that they are worthy of love, and then their perspective of life starts to change. They may notice kindness and love more around them, or they might also start noticing other people's kindness toward them that they couldn't see before.

This is because whatever belief we have, we develop a confirmation bias for that belief. If I believe that it's going to be a crappy day today and I wake up telling myself that today is going to suck, then it might be a very neutral day, but because of my mindset, I'm going to see all the negative things more quickly because my awareness is attuned to this. I'm developing a confirmation bias toward the negative.

However, if I wake up and tell myself that today is going to be a good day and that I'm going to make the most of today, then it could be the same neutral day, but I'm going to see a lot more of the good things because my belief, my outlook is now attuned for me to see things more positively.

The same thing happens for a person who begins to work on creating new beliefs, like when you have someone who has a belief system that they're not lovable, they're going to see this everywhere. For example, they say good morning to a colleague, and their colleague mildly grunts or mumbles back at them; maybe this colleague is having a bad day or is distracted somehow. However, to the individual with the negative belief system that they don't matter, this response affirms that message, and now this message, this belief system becomes stronger.

However, if this individual begins to change their belief system and start telling themselves that they do matter, they are lovable, and that they are important, then they can say good morning to a colleague, and when this colleague mumbles back at them, they are less likely to take it on or take it personally. It doesn't hit home, and they don't internalize it because it's not in line with their belief system. They are now more likely to give that colleague space and question what's going on with them, as opposed to seeing it instantly as a lack in themselves.

When someone is nice to them or pays them a compliment, they are more able to accept the compliment because they actually feel like they deserve the compliment, or the compliment is in line with their internal belief system about themselves. Someone with a negative belief system about themselves might be quicker to dismiss the compliment because it's not in line with their belief that they're worthy of this compliment, whatever that might be.

When you have someone slowly starting to change their belief system, their outlook on the world slowly starts to change, and they will start to see things differently because the way that we make sense of the world is usually in line with our beliefs. When we form a belief about something, we see the things that validate our beliefs. So when we start changing our beliefs, we start to see different things, and that's when our outlook on the world starts to change. Maybe we'll begin to see the world as a kinder place, or we'll begin to form more valuable and meaningful relationships and friendships because now we feel more worthy of those relationships. We might stop sabotaging positive things in our lives because now we feel worthy of them.

So now our values have changed. They've changed because we feel worthy of accepting different things into our lives. And when our values change, then our boundaries change too.

When we let someone take advantage of us because our internal belief system tells us that we don't deserve better treatment, then we allow it to happen precisely because it is in line with our current value system. However, when we value ourselves and believe we are worthy of love, deserve better things, and matter in the world, it becomes easier to set boundaries and confront that individual who treats us poorly. We're less likely to put up with unhealthy behavior and more likely to set healthier boundaries because we've ultimately gone back and changed the core of where that comes from.

It's difficult to change a boundary because it has to come from a place that is much more internal, and so when the values change, that's when the boundaries change too.

Those individuals who are much better able to set healthy boundaries and who don't put up with unhealthy behaviors tend to have confidence in themselves because they know that they shouldn't be treated unfairly. They know that they don't deserve to be treated badly because they have a higher value for themselves. They can stop and evaluate what is acceptable for them and what isn't, and are better able to maintain boundaries because those boundaries are in line with their values. And again, those values ultimately come from their beliefs about themselves.

It's also important to elaborate on the fact that you can reevaluate beliefs, and beliefs can be challenged. Children are sponges and soak everything up, so when parents or other role-model figures who are perceived to know best are the ones telling those children that they'll never amount to anything, then that's exactly what those children's belief systems line up with. This then becomes part of their value system, and this is where behaviors such as self-sabotage come from.

The beautiful thing is that we can reevaluate our beliefs. We can start to reevaluate all the lessons that we learned from our parents and other role models. We can begin to question the messages we were given by our parents and role models, and we can begin to form new beliefs about ourselves.

Our parents and our role models may have given us the messages that we're not worthy or lovable, or that we're not going to amount to anything, or that we're a failure, but we can now go back and reevaluate the fact that our parents or role models didn't know everything. Maybe they were wrong, and because they communicated that you weren't going to amount to anything doesn't mean they were right. Maybe this was communicated from their insecurities, and it doesn't mean that you are a failure.

As an adult who is no longer at the mercy of your authority and role-model figures, you can now determine a new belief pattern, and you can start setting yourself on a path to success and healthier beliefs.

An added point about reevaluating the messages we receive from our role models is that, as adults, we can break away from past messages. As children, we put our lives in our parents' hands, and what they say goes. As children, we believed without question that they knew everything, and they were always right. It's part of how we form our beliefs about the world. However, when we become adults ourselves, and we become our parents' age, that's when we realize that our parents didn't know it all, because we can start to see where our parents were when we are that age.

For example, if your parents had you when they were twenty-five, then when you were five years old and were very impressionable, your parents were thirty. At that time, they're giving you all these beliefs about the world that allow you to make sense of the world, and this is partly how you form your beliefs and outlook. Well, now you're thirty years old and, at that age, you realize holy crap; I don't have a clue about the world! I'm winging it; I'm making stuff up as I go. I have my five-year-old now, and I'm doing the best that I can because this child of mine didn't come with a manual! I'm doing the best that I can, and half the time, I don't know what I'm doing! Now you can go back and see that's also where your parents were.

With all the beliefs that you absorbed about the world when you were a child, now that you're the age where your parents were or maybe even older, you can look back and question what you were told or taught and reevaluate if that rings true for you or not. You can now question if it resonates and choose to accept it as part of your belief system or not. Now you can begin to form your own beliefs and ideas about the world.

Let me emphasize that sometimes, this change only comes from repetition because beliefs can become extremely ingrained. We have our beliefs about the world, and quite often, they become facts. Those beliefs become rigid, and we automatically take those on as true, even when they're not necessarily true.

When we form a belief about the world, it can be flexible. Maybe we can explore our fixed ideas about how we make sense of the world, what we need from the world, where we're going, and what resonates with us. We can begin exploring what our parents told us and reevaluate those lessons.

For example, if your parents told you that you were a failure and weren't going to amount to anything, you can reevaluate this as not true because you know you wouldn't tell your five-year-old that he's a failure, so why would you choose to believe that now when you received the message at five years old? Now, you can begin changing those messages and recognize that you can be successful.

I believe that there's always room for exploration in this regard, especially in a therapeutic setting. If you're reading this and can identify with some of the same negative messages from the past, a counselor can help you reevaluate some of those beliefs. You don't have to be locked into the experiences from your earlier years.

I also want to emphasize something that I see in my work as a therapist, and that's also exactly why I'm writing about it, which is the ripple effect that this concept has. The beliefs that you start with contribute to how you make sense of the world, and this forms your outlook on the world. Your outlook then shapes your values, and this is what influences your boundaries. So, if you want to change your boundaries, you have to change your values. If you want to change your values, you have to change your outlook, your perspective of the world. You change your outlook by changing your beliefs about it, and you change your beliefs by reevaluating what rings true for you and retelling the story behind your life experiences.

7
EXPLANATION VS. EXCUSE

One of the things I've come across a lot in my therapy practice, and with people in general, is that it's a common thing to justify a behavior because they have an explanation for why they did something. They think that justifying a behavior also excuses that behavior. I believe that's a very important distinction to make because a lot of people will justify their actions, especially when they were in the wrong, and they sometimes feel like that explanation excuses that behavior.

Explaining your behavior isn't the same as excusing it.

I think it's important to differentiate between the two because an explanation does not excuse the behavior. When you have someone who did something wrong, and they begin to justify their behavior, you can maybe come to an understanding of where they're coming from or why they engaged in a certain behavior, or made certain choices, but it's important to remember that this still does not necessarily excuse that behavior.

Through my experience, this is a concept that people have struggled with, especially when a person talks about a situation where they have been wronged. They can hear why someone engaged in a certain behavior or even understand the set of circumstances that led a person to make a particular decision, and the situation makes sense, but at the same time, it still doesn't excuse behavior.

I believe it is important to take accountability for actions and behaviors. When you explain a particular behavior, you can see what the different circumstances were that led you to respond in a certain way; however, don't leave it at that. Being able to recognize that a certain set of circumstances led you to make certain decisions allows you to think about some things you can do differently next time so that you don't have to make the same choices again.

When you explain a behavior, quite often, this can be received as an excuse or that you're trying to excuse the behavior. It can be understood *why* certain decisions were made, but sometimes, that doesn't make it okay. I think it's important to create the distinction that, because you can explain something, it doesn't excuse the behavior.

I think this also ties into the realm of forgiveness, and of course, forgiveness is a whole topic in and of itself. I believe that an important aspect of forgiveness is being able to see and understand where someone is coming from, but again, emphasizing this understanding does not excuse the behavior. It doesn't make the behavior okay, and it also doesn't mean forgetting about it or even beginning with a clean slate.

For four and a half years, I worked on a contract providing group therapy and one-on-one sessions in a prison setting. This prison housed almost 3000 male inmates. A lot of people joke that inmates generally say they're innocent, but that was not my experience. Most of the guys I encountered in prison did own up to their crimes, and they did generally take accountability for them, well, at least accountability in the fact that they admitted to their crimes.

However, what I also heard a lot from these same inmates was the explanations for their behaviors. For example, if an inmate had assaulted someone, it was because of a set of circumstances that led them to that moment in time.

In my observation of working with the guys, it felt like because they had solid explanations for behaviors, they also saw their actions as justified. For example, with stories of revenge and an eye for an eye, the outlook was often that if someone wronged them, then they were justified in wronging the person back, etc. These were the justifications and the explanations they would muster to make their behaviors okay.

Understanding someone's pain explains the wound.
It doesn't erase the damage.

If somebody wrongs you, then it's easy to understand why you would wrong or hurt that person back. It even explains why you did it. Well, they hurt me, so I hurt them. However, it still doesn't excuse anything because, in the end, that behavior in itself is not okay.

When you're engaging in revenge tactics and counter-hurting, you're engaging in behavior that you complained about in the other individual. You're now doing the exact same thing, so are you any better? You complain of being hurt, so you hurt someone else. Now you're the same person you complained about!

I want to emphasize here again the distinction between explaining a behavior and excusing a behavior. If you recognize that you're justifying behaviors in some way, even behaviors that are hurtful, unhealthy, or destructive, then you can maybe explain those behaviors in many ways, but does that automatically excuse the behavior and allow that behavior to be okay? No, absolutely not.

When you can understand that your explanation doesn't excuse your behavior, then you can add another layer to that, which is, how can you now go about correcting your behavior?

One question to ask here is, what are you getting out of your behavior, and how can you get your needs met in a healthier way?

For example, take someone who perhaps drinks a lot, and maybe they have a lot of traumas or deep unhappiness, or they're dealing with a lot of things like work or home stress, and they're feeling overwhelmed. Maybe these different external circumstances cause them to want to numb their emotions and feelings of being overwhelmed. They may then justify their alcohol misuse by convincing themselves that they are still functioning by going to work and only drinking in the evening, not in the morning. Or they tell themselves that, of course, they're drinking a lot because they have a lot of stress in their life, and they need this to unwind.

Now, these may all be completely valid points and perfectly understandable explanations for their alcohol misuse, but does that necessarily excuse the behavior?

When behaviors and choices are explained and, therefore, also excused, then that's where the accountability stops. "My drinking is justified, so I'm going to keep doing it." However, when you're able to discern that because you're explaining behavior that doesn't mean you're excusing it, now you can add that extra layer of accountability and take that extra step to identify what is causing the behaviors and choices (e.g. numbing emotions due to stress and providing an escape from dealing with reality) to help explain the drinking.

Because this explanation doesn't excuse the behavior, and because, ultimately, it's destructive, there's room now to explore healthier ways to manage the stressors and the causes of the drinking.

Now, that individual can explore if there are other ways to address stressors in their chaotic family life and maybe take steps to stabilize this chaos more. Or is there a way that they can address work stress and make this more manageable? If there are particular traumas that they are trying to numb, can they begin working on resolving trauma so that alcohol no longer needs to be an outlet?

The other realm in which this manifests a lot is with parenting. This is something I've encountered many times in my counseling practice. In my experience, parents have explained many of their behaviors toward their children, whether the parents are my clients or their now-adult children.

For example, take someone who was abused in some way as a child by their parents. Maybe this abuse was verbal, emotional, or even physical. Once they've worked through their trauma, they may recognize that part of changing their narrative involves acknowledging their parents did the best they could, possibly feeling overwhelmed or repeating cycles of abuse they experienced themselves. Maybe they were role-modeling the behaviors that were demonstrated to them by their parents.

There could be a lot of explanations provided for their behaviors, and indeed, this changing narrative could help the client work toward forgiveness or work toward resolving their trauma, but once again, at no point does this excuse these behaviors in any way.

When we think about explaining away different behaviors, whether it's how our parents were or how we act toward our children, I think it's very important to remember this distinction. I truly believe, and I've seen this a lot in my counseling career, but also specifically working in prison for four and a half years, that excuse and explanation often get lumped together, and therefore, behaviors become justified.

If you treat, e.g., your spouse in a bad way because you're having a bad day, then your spouse can maybe understand that you're having a bad day and this is the reason you're mean to them, but that doesn't mean it's okay to treat your spouse in a bad way.

Another thing I would like to highlight on this subject is that when it comes to upbringing and parenting, we can reevaluate our beliefs about what happened and what we felt was true.

A lot of times, we think that what we're doing is okay because our parents or role models did the same thing, or maybe we learned something from our parents and role models, and therefore, this becomes the truth. However, as children, we're extremely impressionable, and we're like sponges; we soak everything up.

We believed in Santa Claus! We believed that one individual could fly around the Earth in one night and deliver presents to every single child on the planet! We believed this! This was truth for us as children, but whatever crazy explanation we were given, when we questioned the logistics of this, we usually believed this explanation too!

The point is that children will generally believe what is told to them, especially by their authority figures. Children are so impressionable, and this soaking up of information doesn't stop with Santa Claus. It includes all the life lessons from parents and role models; it includes the belief systems of parents and role models. When parents tell children that something is very important and they have to remember that people are like this or the world is like that, children come to see those statements as fact.

Our parents' and role models' truths and the things they instill in us now become our truths.

Another thing I want to share is that you are allowed to go back and reevaluate what is true for you. This is a discussion I've had with many clients, and I've worked with clients to help them reevaluate their own truths. because their parents and authority figures instill the belief that the world is scary, dangerous, and full of bad people, it doesn't mean this has to become their truth or experience.

I know I have already written about this in a previous chapter, so I won't spend too much time on this subject here but I wanted to tie in that the way different individuals have explained their behaviors to you doesn't necessarily either excuse their behaviors, nor does it have to become your own truth.

When it comes to differentiating between explaining a behavior and excusing a behavior, it's important for both the victim and the perpetrator to make this distinction. It is sometimes hard for victims to work through their experiences because of the way that explaining behaviors is often paired and lumped together with excusing the behavior. But it is equally important for the perpetrator to make this distinction also because only in this way can accountability and change happen.

The only way that accountability can happen is through this distinction. Every negative, wrongful, and hurtful action can be explained. Most people do have a sound explanation for unwanted behaviors, but accountability can never happen if this also provides an excuse.

By not making the distinction, what you're, in effect, saying is that you would do the same thing again given the same set of circumstances. Accountability is about recognizing that behaviors can be wrong and justified *despite* the circumstances.

For example, if someone has something that you want but it's theirs and not yours, you may still feel like you have a right to it and that possibly you've worked as much as they have, or maybe you've even worked harder. You may tell yourself that you're a better person than they are and that you deserve this thing more. All of these things explain your motives for why you end up taking this thing, whatever that may be, but it also takes away your accountability in that what you did was inherently justified, and even with all the rationale, it still wasn't okay because in the end it wasn't yours to take.

When you lump explanation and excuse together, then you justify why you did a wrongful behavior because you can explain it. But this is precisely the thinking error, and this is what I am highlighting.

You can heal without excusing what hurt you.

8

THE OBJECTIVE LENS

One thing that I see quite often from my counseling experience is that when you're in the middle of a situation, it's sometimes very difficult to be objective in it. When you are emotionally connected to a situation–whether it's a relationship, work stress, or anything else–it's very hard to see things objectively.

This may sound like a simple concept, but it's still a recurring theme in counseling, and that's why I decided to write about it.

One of the things that I see a lot is, for example, when clients come in because they're in a certain situation and they don't know what to do. They want to ask me for advice, or they want me to tell them what to do because they're stuck in a situation. As a counselor, it's not my role to give advice. Instead, I'm going to allow the client to explore their own thoughts and feelings so that the client can decide themselves about what is right for them.

I'm not the client, so if I were to give advice on what I think is best, then ultimately, my advice comes from my perspective, and I would give advice based on what I would think is best for me in that situation. This, however, may not be the best advice for the client in their particular situation.

As counselors, it's very important for us to not give advice or tell somebody what to do. It's our responsibility to allow clients to explore the different possibilities for themselves so they can come up with their own decisions on what they need to do in the situation they're stuck in.

There is one thing that I will say here, and maybe I'll get some slack for saying this, but I'm going to say it anyway, reiterating that I'm writing this from my experience, which is what I'm sharing with you.

When it comes to a decision that is between the head and the heart, the decision that is made with the head and not the heart is generally the best decision. There, I said it.

I know that this goes against such popular belief, especially when you think of Hollywood and the message to follow your heart and make these reckless decisions because it feels like a good idea at the time. But I can tell you that it seems to me, in my overall experience, that when someone makes these kinds of impulsive decisions based on their emotions, it's not always the best idea.

Making drastic decisions without having thought them through, in my experience, does not always lead to the right outcomes.

Of course, I'm not talking 100% of the time, and this rule of thumb is not always the case. I know there are many people who will testify that they made impulsive decisions that went against everything they thought was rational and the outcome turned out well. I do believe those might be in the minority, though.

I've generally witnessed that the times when people have made very drastic and different decisions, those decisions have been accompanied by a lot of thought about the situation. They've typically engaged in a lot of planning, and weighing pros and cons, advantages and disadvantages, consequences and such things.

I've noticed that even when clients make big decisions that appear to be emotionally based, there's usually a fair amount of thought that has gone into it.

**Big emotions are real.
But they aren't always great decision-makers.**

For example, I had a client quit a job without going to a different job. This may seem like an impulsive decision, but this particular client actually put a lot of thought into this decision. It definitely wasn't the "I hate this job, so I'm leaving" decision. No, this client had been with this job for many years, and through the process of therapy, he realized how much of the toxicity of his job seeped into his everyday life. He realized that for his emotional well-being, he needed to leave. He felt paralyzed from being able to move forward with the career endeavors he wanted to pursue, and this is why he quit this job. Even though on the surface it may have seemed like it, it wasn't reckless or impulsive at all.

When you feel stuck, and you don't know what to do, there are a couple of different ways to approach this. The first approach is to ride it out. So basically, if you're feeling confused, or no decision seems like the right decision and you have no idea what to do, maybe the rule of thumb here is to not make any decisions at that time. If no decision feels right, then maybe that's because, at that moment, no decision is right.

Maybe in that situation, waiting will provide more information and clarity or less heightened emotions, and a confident decision can be made with time.

For example, if you're in a bad work environment and you don't have anywhere to go, you don't have another job lined up, or you don't know what you would do financially if you were to quit that job, but you also know that the job makes you miserable then it feels like a no-win situation.

If you go to work, you're miserable, but if you quit your job, you'd be stressed, so it doesn't matter what you do; it's not going to feel good. Then maybe the rule of thumb at this time is to not make any decisions in that moment, but instead sit with your emotional experience and allow yourself to go through that for a while to allow some clarity to form.

With that clarity or detaching from the emotional experience, you might be better able to make a decision that feels a little clearer, or that makes more sense.

> When you're in it, you can't always see it.

Another approach to problem-solving a situation where no outcome feels right, and you feel stuck, is to take yourself out of the picture and put it on someone more objective. For example, a friend, sibling, or some extended family. If they came up to you in your position, what would be some of the advice you'd give them, based on what you're seeing about the situation?

Going back to the working example, hypothetically speaking, you're not happy in your job, and you experience all the things mentioned above from the scenario, and you feel completely stuck about what decision to make about it. Now, imagine your sister is in this situation, and your sister has this job that makes her miserable every day. What would you say to her? What advice would you have for her? What course of action would you tell her to take?

When you see your situation objectively, and you can see it from the outside and imagine someone else going through the same thing, how would you problem-solve it now? What are some things in your sister's situation that become priorities?

If I told you to take your emotions out of the experience and to think rationally, this would be both an unfair and unrealistic expectation because you are the subjective experiencer of this situation, and by default, this comes with the emotional experience attached.

However, if you remove the emotion by imagining the situation is happening to someone else and you are now advising them, you might start to problem-solve in ways you couldn't see before.

This is one way to minimize being emotionally connected to that situation. I feel like it's important to reiterate that emotions are very important, and as I've already written about before, we need our emotions to guide us. What I'm talking about here is the tendency to *only* consider our emotional experience while neglecting reason and logic and then making decisions that are later regretted.

So, if your brother or sister came to you and asked you what you would do in their situation, instead of telling them they should quit their job or find another job, you might come up with other solutions like exploring the aspects of the job that are making the work environment very difficult. There might be more room for exploration, which requires the use of increased logic and reasoning.

Your sister (you) may identify that the work hours are awful, or maybe your boss is incredibly negative, or maybe you don't get along with certain colleagues. It could be that the work demands themselves are overwhelming or that there's too much negative gossip going around. So an increased emotional detachment can lead to a greater exploration of what aspects lead you to feeling overwhelmed at work. This, in turn, can lead you to problem-solve those particular areas instead of working as a whole.

For example, if you're feeling overloaded by the actual work demands, maybe you could have a conversation with your boss about moving around some responsibilities or prioritizing tasks. If you're experiencing difficult colleagues, then you may implement different interpersonal effectiveness skills to improve communication and foster those relationships, or seek out more positive colleagues and spend more time and energy with those who make you feel better instead of worse.

Or if your boss is way too demanding, maybe you can approach their boss and let them know how your boss is affecting you, or if your work hours are causing stress, then maybe you can request or negotiate different work hours.

Even though the responses may not necessarily give you the desired result or some of these approaches may not be feasible, the point is when you're able to emotionally detach from a difficult situation and look at it more objectively, you can also problem-solve a little more clearly and come up with different types of solutions.

For example, if the job is all-around bad and you're looking for ways to get out of it rather than improve specific aspects of your job, then maybe it's about considering what the possibilities are that are out there, and putting out some job applications, or starting that process.

What would you advise your sibling to do? Maybe you'd tell them that you've noticed that they're miserable in their job and advise them that it's time to start looking for something else. And how would they be able to do that? Are they tired every single day? And if so, would you suggest that maybe on Saturdays, once they've slept longer and feel more refreshed, they commit to putting in three job applications that day?

Whatever advice you'd give to a friend, a sibling, or a relative in that situation, essentially, that's the advice you'd give yourself because, in the end, you're looking at their situation from your perspective. This is why counselors can't give advice, but it's also why you can give yourself the best advice - when you're in problem-solving mode!

The thing is, when we're emotionally attached to a situation, we're more likely to make emotional decisions. However, a lot of times, those emotional decisions are more impulsive decisions rather than being thought out, and the thought-out decisions tend to be better.

Now, the ideal decision is a decision that is well thought out and where the emotions back that up. This is why the presence of both emotions and reasoning is important.

When you make a decision, and it's a thought-out decision, but it feels good as well, and it feels like the right decision, then that's the ideal decision because the emotions and reasoning are in synch.

Something that I've seen a lot of, in the realm of impulsivity and the context of relationships, is that relationships that start very intensely tend to fizzle out pretty intensely also. I've seen individuals glamorize their partners when they've barely met, and quite often, they feel like the height and the intensity of the relationship is their baseline, but I've seen those same relationships go downhill very fast; in some cases, they crash and burn.

I've also noticed that the relationships that begin more stable and steadier, where more of a foundation and especially a friendship is built, tend to be the relationships that last.

I've also seen this pattern with big life decisions. I've seen people say screw this, I don't like this, and they quit and make decisions because they're angry at the moment. They cut people out of their lives because of anger toward them, and they're potentially ruining a good friendship or relationship where a lot of misunderstandings could have been resolved with simple communication, compassion, and listening.

I've encountered numerous clients who have not spoken to close family members for literally years because of one argument. I've encountered clients who quit their jobs because they were feeling overwhelmed in one moment, and in every one of these situations, emotion, not reasoning, was the primary decision maker.

One thing that I want to emphasize is that when you have the urge to make a very impulsive decision, based on your heightened emotion in that moment, the rule of thumb is don't make that decision! Begin by riding out the intensity of your emotion and work through managing that first.

One thing that I can tell you with confidence is that whatever intensity of emotion you're feeling at any given moment, that intensity is not going to last.

If you're feeling very angry with someone, at the moment, that intensity of anger that you're feeling in that very moment will fade. Guaranteed. You cannot sustain the strength of any emotion for any extended period. Now, you might still be angry at the person for a while, and you might feel upset or wronged, but what I'm talking about is the *intensity* of that particular emotion. I'm talking about the force of that anger that makes you want to blow up at the moment, explode, and cause you to make reckless decisions.

When I have conversations about what people should do in a situation where they feel very stuck, or they feel intensely about something, the first thing is to ride out the intensity of the emotions. I'm willing to bet that whatever decision you're planning on making, doing it during the force of that emotion, is probably going to be the worst time to make that decision.

This is something that can even be referred to in an earlier chapter where I talk about what happens in the brain with the limbic system and the prefrontal cortex. What happens in the brain with very heightened emotions is that you're not accessing your reasoning capacity because you're making decisions from the limbic system, which is the emotional seat of the brain. This leads to very impulsive decisions because when you make any decision based solely on emotion, and you don't access the reasoning part of your brain that lies in the prefrontal cortex, then you're also not thinking of consequences.

In that moment you don't have the reasoning capacity to recognize that if you make a decision, then it will lead to X, which leads to Y which leads to Z. You can't recognize that maybe Z is not a good place to end up so to prevent Z from happening, you have to refrain from the impulsive decision to begin with and revise your action strategy. This is what you need your reasoning capacity for.

When you feel stuck in a situation, it's because you're emotionally connected to it, and then it's difficult to see your situation from a logical perspective because your emotions get clouded in it. When you take yourself out of the picture and then place it on someone else, you're more likely to approach the same situation in a more level-headed way. You're going to be able to see more of the facts of the situation, brainstorm questions, and problem-solve different aspects of your situation.

With an emotional detachment, you're going to be better able to determine the next steps and consequences of each decision and each possible outcome, as opposed to seeing something that is emotionally charged, which can lead to a perspective like "you know what, I don't care about that."

An emotionally attached and charged perspective might make you more likely to tell yourself you'll figure it out when you get there, but that might not be a good thing because it might be important for you to know what the next steps are now.

Here's a classic example and something I've experienced with one of my clients who was in a domestic violence relationship. This relationship was horrible and physically abusive, and my client's self-esteem was barely existent, if at all. She was very much in the domestic violence cycle, had a long history of substance abuse, and had been taken advantage of by all sorts of men from a very early age. When I saw her, she was in a violent relationship, and as is typical of these types of relationships, she didn't know whether to stay or to leave.

One day, she was in my office, and she was talking about her relationship and how she was with her partner, who had physically abused her. We were talking about her safety; nobody deserves to be treated this way, this is not okay, etc. It's a very interesting phenomenon because you can say many of the rational things, but when someone is very much in this abusive cycle, it's so difficult for them to see it because of the amount of emotional attachment that's present in the relationship.

My client was making excuses for him and giving all the reasons why she should stay in the relationship, and how things would get better, etc. As a counselor, this is a very challenging type of client because, no matter what you say, it's almost like you simply cannot get through.

So, I asked her what she would do if it were her sister who came to her, saying that her partner had beaten her up and always promised things would get better, but they never did. What if her sister was sitting next to her with these bruises, telling her that she felt she should stay in the relationship? And with no hesitation whatsoever, my client said: "Well, I would tell her to leave! She'd have to get out!"

It was as clear as day to her that she would tell her sister to get out of this relationship, yet she couldn't do it herself.

This concept of taking yourself out of the picture to remove the emotional attachment and to gain clarity may sound like a no-brainer - a very simple concept, but the only reason I chose to add this chapter and talk about it is that even with its simplicity, it's a very prevalent theme and one which recurs frequently in my sessions.

9
REFRAMING PROBLEMS

This chapter will talk about how to reframe problems to make them more manageable, as sometimes it's our minds that work against us and cause us to feel stuck.

One of the exercises I used to do with inmates when I ran groups in the prison system was to get them into small groups and make them come up with definitions of different words in the realm of problems, e.g., what is the definition of a problem, a challenge, a solution, an obstacle, etc.

One of the more interesting debates that we would frequently have was to identify the difference between a problem and a challenge. What distinguishes a problem from a challenge? They seem like the same thing, and in many ways that one can be defined, so can the other, e.g., a problem is some kind of obstacle that presents itself. Well, a challenge can be defined in the same way.

When it comes to a problem and a challenge, the actual situation is the same. The thing that turns a problem into a challenge is that your approach to it changes. It's not the situation or definition that changes, but you that changes because you change your approach to it.

The thing with a challenge is that it's like a will, a resolve, a motivation to overcome. A challenge presents with it an air, a determination to overcome, like telling yourself how you'll overcome rather than if you'll overcome. A challenge is more about what you need to do to get through it, rather than seeing that there's a problem in front of you.

If there's a problem in front of you, then that's the obstacle in itself. But when there's a challenge in front of you, the added piece to it is about determining how to overcome this obstacle. When something is deemed either a problem or a challenge, nothing about the facts of the situation changes. It's the energy of the situation that changes. It's the mindset about it that changes. And that's the difference.

Say, for example, you work in retail, and you often encounter customers who are rude or negative, or who like to complain. Let's say your customer base is a very difficult type of customer. Well, that's a problem because it affects your mood and outlook on your job; it tests your patience, how you feel about showing up for work every day, and how exhausted you feel at the end of every day. So you've identified your customer base as a problem.

However, when you change the word "problem" into "challenge," and you see your difficult customer base as a challenge, then it's almost like you're telling yourself: "Bring it on! I'm going to see what I can do to take this challenge on and overcome this!" It almost brings with it a conviction to try to implement your diplomacy and communication skills to the max to see how well you can work with these difficult customers!

The energy about this situation has now shifted because your approach toward it has changed. This shift is huge. It makes a tremendous amount of difference because, and I emphasize this again, the problem in front of you has never changed. The only thing that changed is your newfound perspective on the situation.

> **The energy of the situation shifts the moment your perspective does.**

Whenever you find yourself in a situation where you encounter a problem, and you're identifying the problem, then one of the most effective ways to reframe that problem is to turn it into a challenge.

Turning problems into challenges includes a shift in perspective. It starts with identifying a problem and working toward a solution-focused mindset. There could be so many creative ways to solve problems. There could be so many types of problems, be they work situations or relationships, but this can also even apply to normal everyday life situations.

You can apply this to something as simple as what to make for dinner. You may come home and think, "Ugh, there's nothing to eat in the house!" That's a problem! But when you see something seemingly small as a challenge, you may challenge yourself to find all the different random ingredients from your pantry and put them together to make a meal!

When things become challenges and not problems, you're not focusing on the obstacle part of the problem. Instead, you're seeing the outcome, and your focus is on how to get there. The obstacle itself is no longer the focus - the outcome is. It's about the way to the outcome.

If you have an eight-foot wall in front of you, you can identify this as an obstacle. You can tell yourself that your journey stops here because the wall is in the way. But when the wall becomes a challenge, you don't stop your journey; instead, you brainstorm ways to get over the wall.

A challenge is a conviction of your overcoming, your ability. This is a beautiful thing because it changes your entire approach. Like I said, it could be big things but also seemingly small matters. So when you identify the problems in your life, I challenge you (!) to reframe these into challenges and see if this shifts your perspective and your approach to the matter.

A challenge almost has an air of excited anticipation. Bring it on! I can do this! What do you have for me? It becomes almost playful, like it takes the negativity out of it. When faced with a problem, sometimes the mindset is that we can't do it, or there's a sense of burden attached. We feel a heaviness, something negative, a nuisance of sorts. But with the lightness and playfulness of a challenge, we can brainstorm how we're going to overcome this, and there's an energy shift that attaches to a challenge. This energy and conviction allow you to turn this into a motivation to get to the outcome rather than be stuck.

Now, take someone who experiences symptoms of anxiety, say social anxiety, that causes a great deal of stress being around groups of individuals. Maybe their thoughts are negatively going into overdrive, and they have a difficult time navigating everyday situations because their anxiety is taking over. This, of course, is a problem.

The anxiety can even increase in anticipation of having anxiety, so it creates this snowball effect sometimes. So, when these clients begin to reframe this anxiety problem as a challenge, it can sometimes help the approach. For example, going into a situation and asking themselves how they are going to make the best of this situation.

For example, say your boss tells you that they would like you to present on a certain topic to the team at the next staff meeting, and the team is a pretty good size. It can be a little intimidating to be put on the spot like that. With added anxiety about speaking in front of others, now you're faced with a problem. You may experience negative thoughts like, "Ugh, why did my boss ask me to do this? I don't want to do this. I'm going to make a fool of myself. It's going to be awful."

However, when you reframe this into a challenge, what you're saying is, "How am I going to do this? How am I going to make the best of this? How am I going to present myself in a way that is engaging?" The existence of the outcome doesn't even come into question.

In this situation, you have now been challenged to present this topic in front of your team, so instead of approaching it with heaviness and a sense of burden because it's something you have to do, you ask yourself how you can do this and do it well. You begin to wonder how you may be present in front of your team and do a good job. When you reframe things in this way, you add motivation; you add energy; you add problem-solving. You become goal-oriented and outcome-oriented, and you go beyond the problem.

Now, the outcome, the matter of speaking in front of your team, becomes the focus. The end result becomes inevitable, and instead of wondering if the outcome is even a possibility, the question becomes one of how.

There are several other ways to reframe problems. So far, I've discussed one reframe, which is turning a problem into a challenge, but there are many more. This chapter is about how to reframe problems so that you're not caught up in the negativity of them or that you don't stay stuck in the obstacle part, but rather it's about overcoming the situation.

Hidden in every obstacle is an invitation to grow.

So, the first reframe is turning a problem into a challenge. The second reframe is to look for the opportunity in the situation. One of the things I feel is important to mention is that when a problem presents itself, it's okay to have an initial emotional response. For example, if you've been excited about something for a long time, and the thing you've been looking forward to gets canceled or doesn't happen, then it's completely appropriate to be disappointed.

Experiencing something like a letdown or a cancellation after excitement is a disappointing thing to go through, so the immediate emotions that follow are very much okay.

Another example could be someone else placing more responsibilities on you when you feel overwhelmed already, and you become annoyed and irritated by that, maybe even angry. Well, be annoyed! Be irritated! That would be an irritating situation! Those feelings would be very appropriate and understandable.

Those initial emotional responses to frustrations and problems are completely appropriate, and there's definitely a time and place to allow those emotions to exist. I don't want to dismiss those initial emotional responses because I think they are important and extremely valid.

One of the main points I'm trying to convey in this chapter is the importance of not getting stuck in a negative emotional response. This is about how not to get stuck in the negative emotions of anger, frustration, stress, and whatever other emotions that don't feel good.

So yes, absolutely experience the initial emotions that come from experiencing the problem, but don't get stuck there.

This second reframe, when it comes to working through problems, is finding opportunities in the different problems. Here is a great default question you can ask yourself, "What is the opportunity that presents itself in this problem?"

You may need to look for it, or maybe you have to be creative to find some opportunity, but I'm willing to bet that the vast majority of the time, there is an opportunity that comes out of a negative situation. Even if you're not sure what that opportunity might be, a lot of times, it falls into the realm of testing your strength, testing your capabilities, showing others what you can do, or showing others your strength.

For example, I'll go back to the work example of your boss wanting you to present in front of your team and you absolutely don't want to do this. You may feel all those initial negative emotions, such as stress, anxiety, feeling overwhelmed, etc., and that's perfectly appropriate.

Once you've worked through those initial emotional responses, then you can reframe your perspective about the situation and ask yourself, "What opportunity does this situation present for me?"

It could be an opportunity to present your competence to your team. Or it could be an opportunity for you to show your confidence or to demonstrate your hard work. It could be that you do good work, and this is the opportunity to show that you make an effort to do good work and that you display professional integrity.

It could even be to show your boss what you're capable of, to show your strengths to your boss. If you're thinking of wanting to move up in the company or do something different within the company, then doing something favorable like this may help you get there because other people are seeing more of your strengths.

A lot of good things might come out of this situation. Another opportunity that may happen in a situation like this is that it may strengthen your confidence. If you put work into preparing for your presentation and then you do well and receive positive feedback, then after the presentation, you may feel so much better about your ability and confidence levels. You may recognize that you have a greater capacity for pushing yourself out of your comfort zone, which increases your confidence and courage to do other things you may not have tried before.

Yet another area wherein you may find opportunities is in areas of failure. Maybe you set out to do something, and you didn't quite make it, then perhaps you begin engaging in negative self-talk, like telling yourself you're a failure. Why would I ever try this again? On the other hand, you can find an opportunity in it.

The question to highlight the opportunity is: how can you learn from that experience and thereby grow from that experience?

This is very important, too, because quite often, we lose confidence with failure. For example, if you're taking a test and fail, it's easy to lose confidence in your ability to pass this test or even want to try again. You may even question your ability as a whole. However, if you take a test and fail, you can learn from it and grow stronger from that when you identify what aspects of the test you were good at and weren't.

By exploring this, you know what areas to study more, and then you can focus on those particular areas, grow your strengths, and have a better chance of passing the test next time. Research even shows that we learn more from failure than we do from success.

One very popular example that most people already know about is Thomas Edison and his discovery of the lightbulb. I believe it took him about 10,000 tries, and what Edison learned was that with every failure, there was one more way of how not to create the lightbulb, which kept narrowing down how to successfully create a lightbulb because he was continuously learning from all the ways that didn't work!

There's so much learning that happens in a process like this. We learn a lot about what doesn't work from failure, and we can take away as much knowledge from what doesn't work as from what does work.

Say, for example, you want to try something new, so you begin a new project or a new undertaking, and you set your mind to doing it well. But when it all crumbles and fades and it ends up being a disaster, then that whole experience ultimately has been a learning curve. That experience has now become an opportunity for you to discover what your strengths are because you understand your strengths better when you also know what your strengths are not! The experience has narrowed that down.

Instead of seeing the whole experience as a failure filled with regret and your negative self-talk telling you that you shouldn't have done this ("What was I thinking?"), it's more about reframing this perspective and identifying the opportunity within this.

You can ask yourself what you have learned through the experience. It could be that your knowledge of the project was not sufficient, or that you rushed into wanting the outcome and rushed through the groundwork, or it could be that you needed extra support that you were too stubborn to accept, or maybe you assumed how something should have worked out, or whatever else the case might have been.

The thing is, whatever mistakes you make throughout the process, you're unlikely to make those same mistakes again. Your knowledge becomes stronger and better when you pursue the same project next time.

Instead of seeing things as failures, I challenge you to reframe your perspective and see them as opportunities for learning. To quote Desmond Tutu: "I never fail. I either win, or I learn."

I want to reiterate that this is not the same as dismissing the feelings associated with failure. Emotions that come with failure, including disappointment, anger at yourself, and feelings of loss that come with failure, are all extremely valid feelings. The point I am emphasizing here is not to get stuck there because that's the thing that causes negative and resentful outlooks.

Absolutely, be disappointed if an endeavor or a project didn't work out. Be angry at yourself if you can't do what you set out to do, but don't get stuck there. Work through those emotions, allow yourself to experience and validate those emotions, and then reframe your perspective to identify opportunities for better and more effective learning in the future. This is how you become more successful at something you struggled with initially.

To review, when it comes to the first two reframes of problems, the first one is to turn problems into challenges, and the second one is to identify the opportunities presented in those problems.

The third reframe to address problems is that sometimes they become a little easier to manage when you apply meaning to them.

This doesn't necessarily have to be in a spiritual/higher purpose type of way; however, if that is part of your belief system and you can draw strength by adding a spiritual meaning, then absolutely yes, draw strength from that.

You can also apply meaning to different situations, even when you don't necessarily believe in something higher or that there's a higher purpose in life. It's almost a similar concept to finding opportunity in problems, but finding meaning is more about making a problem easier to cope with if you know there is meaning attached to it.

It's almost like a sequence of events that leads to a reframing of your outlook; the first step is to see that the problem you face has a meaning and purpose attached, which changes your approach to the problem. It allows the problem to exist, and so your approach changes from rejecting the problem or telling yourself the problem shouldn't exist to one of addressing the problem.

The second step is to identify what meaning your problem has, and this is done by asking yourself what possible opportunity you can gain from the problem in front of you. The third step is reframing the problem as a challenge, as you've now identified the meaning and opportunity in it.

For example, if you face many challenges at work, such as starting a new job as a mental health counselor and getting all the challenging clients in your first few months, you might go to work every day feeling unsure. This could coincide with questioning your competency and skills, making you feel like the biggest impostor.

However, when you reframe your perspective to add meaning to this situation, you ask yourself what purpose this could serve. You may identify that as a novice being thrown into the deep end, it better equips you for dealing with challenging clients in the future because you've been able to work through this. It doesn't change the workload, but the reframe can make it easier to deal with.

If everything is easy and things go smoothly, we're never challenged, and we never have a testimony to our strengths. Say, for example, someone displays aggression and violence, and as a result of destructive behavior while driving with road rage, they have to go to anger management classes. They go through the classes and learn healthier outlets for managing anger, and they also work on applying these skills. After a while, they believe they have a handle on their anger, and they are now in control of their behaviors.

Then, one day, they feel angry while driving home, and as soon as they get over into a lane, cars clear out. When they get to a stoplight, the light conveniently turns green right as they approach it. Nobody cuts them off, and everyone is driving courteously. The roads are clear, and nobody is driving slowly in the fast lane.

Now this individual comes home, and they tell themselves holy crap, I didn't experience any road rage at all! I guess I did get a handle on my anger!

But did they, though?

The problem is that they never could demonstrate their anger management skills because everything was easy. If this individual reframes their self-talk to view annoying drivers as an opportunity to demonstrate anger management skills, the problem becomes a challenge to test their abilities.

Now, if they hit every red light on their way home and they are becoming increasingly frustrated, this reframes the meaning of those red lights, and this becomes an opportunity to practice, e.g., patience.

Ultimately, this individual is not going to know if they did learn to manage their behaviors when angry unless they are put into situations where they can apply their anger management skills and demonstrate these and use them successfully.

The way you apply meaning to problems is that the more problems you face now, the easier your future problems become because you develop experience in problem-solving.

A lot of strength can be drawn when meaning comes from the realm of higher purpose and spirituality. For example, there might be someone who believes in reincarnation who faces one negative situation after another, and who experiences a lot of stressors. This particular individual may have an easier time managing these stressors if the meaning they attach to their situation is that every time they overcome one of these obstacles, they are clearing out karma, which means they are setting themselves up for a better and easier life in their next life.

Another example is someone who has Christian beliefs, and they may believe that God doesn't give you anything more than you can handle. They may believe that God has a plan for situations, and the individual doesn't necessarily know what that plan is. So, when a stressful event does happen, or they experience an upsetting situation, this can be eased with the belief that this is happening for a reason, and they can put their faith in that. This belief makes them better able to manage their situation simply because they have applied meaning to it.

This is why applying meaning to difficult situations can be incredibly important. When you reframe your thoughts in this way, the problems seem to become more manageable because the outlook changes from focusing on the problem to focusing on the purpose of the problem.

Again, the meaning you give to situations doesn't have to come from the realm of spirituality. It could be anything you apply; it's only limited by your thoughts, which can be endless. It's like making sense of a situation and maybe even allowing that problem to exist.

The other thing that happens is that this reframe gets you into problem-solving mode. You don't stay stuck on thoughts such as, "This shouldn't be happening," "This problem shouldn't exist," "I shouldn't have to deal with this!" It gets you out of the shoulda/woulda/coulda's (also known in the mental health realm as stinkin' thinkin') to asking yourself what you need to do to work through the problem.

Attaching meaning to problems can increase motivation to work through the problem simply because a purpose has been attached to it.

These three reframes to problems come up a lot in my counseling practice because, of course, clients come to counseling often precisely because they are facing major obstacles and different stressors in their lives. These stressors can range from significant breakups and job losses to poor communication and adjustment to new environments. Once clients validate and process their emotions, they can shift to problem-solving by reframing issues as challenges, finding opportunities, and adding meaning and purpose to their experiences.

10

LEARN TO LISTEN

Several things I'd like to talk about in this chapter are the importance of validation, the challenge of validating others, and why not to be so quick to judge others or to have a response because these are very consistent things I see regularly. I see this in my counseling practice, definitely in the context of relationship counseling, but also within the general public.

This particular topic is the one thing I see that creates so much conflict. The sheer inability to validate someone's experience is so prevalent and that's why I feel the need to talk about this.

Validation is about allowing someone to have their experience, whether that's their thoughts, their feelings or belief systems, or their perspective of the world. Whatever experience someone else has, validating is allowing that person to have it.

Here's the thing about validation: to validate someone's experience, you don't need to agree. This is the beautiful thing about validation. You can validate someone else's experience and that doesn't mean that you're agreeing with them or that you're conforming to their viewpoint. You're not conforming to their beliefs or perspectives when you validate them. You're not changing your belief and "giving in" to their belief when you validate.

I wonder if this is the misconception that makes it difficult for people to apply validation because, in my experience, a lot of people are unable to validate others and then ultimately get into a power struggle. This happens when an individual has their thoughts and beliefs, their opinions and outlook, and then someone else has a different outlook than them. One common perception is that if I have a perspective on something and I feel I'm right, and your perspective is different, then you must be wrong.

This is where the power struggle comes in, where the conflict comes in. In my experience, people struggle with the concept of allowing someone else to have their own thoughts and beliefs when they're different from their beliefs.

To be able to apply validation, you don't have to have the same beliefs and opinions as the other person.

I often have to challenge people to not be so quick to form judgments about things because that's their perspective. Someone else might have an idea about what works for them, but that doesn't necessarily mean it works for others. What works for one person doesn't always work for another person because everyone has their own life experiences. Everyone has their own strengths, likes, dislikes, etc. Everybody is uniquely different.

One observation I've made, is when people are not able to validate others, and it turns into conflict. One thing I see, especially in the context of relationships, is the inability to listen. When someone's experiences and feelings are invalidated, the immediate response is for that person to justify their feelings and beliefs. My challenge for them is to bite their tongue, hold back for a second, and not be so quick to justify their actions and feelings, but to sit and listen to the other person.

Judging others based on your own perspective is one of the biggest barriers to connection.

In most of these instances, the person is not actually hearing what the other is saying. They have difficulty stepping back from their own need to talk about their own experience, and thereby, they don't allow the other person to have their experience. This takes a willingness to understand the other person's perspective. It takes a willingness to see where the other person is coming from.

This dynamic comes back in so many variations, and it comes back to the idea that if someone sees something from their own perspective, then that perspective is right. They form an opinion about something based on their perspective, and now that opinion is right. This means they also form an opinion about what someone else should or shouldn't do based on that very limited perspective.

This observation may sound very naive and simple, but that is the context of what I see happening over and over again. I see people form major judgments about situations they know absolutely nothing about. It could be something as simple as someone calling out from work on a day because they were sick, and immediately, they have colleagues forming judgments about whether they're actually sick or not. These colleagues may make up whole reasons for why this colleague took the day off, none of which are based in reality.

If you find that your mind tends to go down a trail of assumptions and you jump to conclusions about situations where you don't have all the facts, then whoa, take a step back! You don't know anything about the situation and have immediately formed an opinion about it! Instead of invalidating that colleague's day off and thinking they're probably out with friends for the day or whatever narrative you've told yourself, just maybe, they are actually sick!

Validating is about allowing a different situation than your own to exist. For example, if you've experienced a similar stressor but it wasn't a big deal to you, you may think someone else is exaggerating, overreacting, or being dramatic. However, what you're not doing is acknowledging that this stressor that wasn't a big deal to you may actually be a big deal to someone else.

Here's another thing that happens in my experience and observations. People's responses to different situations are so very different. Five different people can have the same experience, and all five people can take away very different memories from their experience because of the meaning they've applied to their experiences. It's like seeing two small children in the playground and they're both running around and playing. Then, they both accidentally fall and scrape their knees. One child may giggle, get up, and play with their friends again while the other child starts bawling because their scraped knee is a much scarier experience for them than it is for the other child.

They both fell and hurt their knees in the exact same way, and the level of pain was the same, but their subjective experience of the fall was very different.

In the same way, because you don't have the same reaction doesn't mean that another person's reaction is invalid. I wish that more people could grasp this idea of someone having an experience, but because you don't experience it the same way doesn't mean that this experience is invalid for the other person. It's such an important concept because it carries over in so many ways. There's so much conflict that comes from this one concept of people not being able to validate other people's experiences.

We tend to be so quick to see things from our own perspective, and we're so quick to judge. We're so quick to make assumptions about situations, and we're so quick to tell others what they should or shouldn't do or how they should or shouldn't feel.

We have no idea. We don't know what someone else's subjective experience is; we only see our side of the situation. We don't know what impressions other people form of the world, and we don't have the same life experiences, so who are we to tell someone what to do, or to make assumptions about someone else's life?

Yet we do it all the time. I think a big part of it is that one of the things we're notoriously bad at is allowing someone else to have their experience. For example, say someone has gone through a major breakup with someone who wasn't good for them, but they're still so upset about the breakup, then they're still allowed to be upset about it. Maybe everyone else around that person tells them they should be happy that person is gone, or they deserve better, etc. However, that person is still allowed to feel devastated, and if that person is feeling devastated, then by default, for the fact that they are experiencing these upset feelings, that feeling of devastation is valid.

You may have gone through a significant breakup also, and instead of being devastated, you feel relieved because the person who left was awful anyway, and you may not have been particularly affected by the breakup. Naturally, you may be more inclined to tell the other person that they're so much better without the person and that they should forget about them, etc. Maybe all these things are true. However, this feedback is neither helpful to that person, nor does it validate their experience. You're not allowing this person to have their feelings about their breakup.

This is the pattern that happens a lot in conflict. One individual could be talking about how they feel, and the response is that those feelings are stupid, or they shouldn't feel like that. Because one person can't relate or doesn't experience the same emotions, they tell the other that they shouldn't feel like that. What that person is not doing is validating those feelings.

One thing that I can tell you about emotions is by default, for the very fact that they exist, this makes them valid. If someone is upset about something, their being upset is valid for the simple fact that they are feeling this. If someone is excited about something and you don't care about the thing they're excited about, the person's excitement is still valid for the simple reason that they're feeling excited.

If you were to feel indifferent about the same situation, your feeling of indifference is also valid. You may wonder why someone is excited over something that feels insignificant to you, while they may question your indifference, thinking it's an exciting event. What both of you are not doing here is you're not allowing each other to have your personal emotional experience.

One of the things that I want to emphasize in this chapter is the importance of validation. Simply the importance of allowing someone to have their own experience about something. People are entitled to their own thoughts, opinions, and beliefs, no matter what it is.

This is an important place to be reminded that feelings and behaviors are two very separate things. No matter what anyone is feeling, those feelings are valid, no matter what the feeling is. Now what that person *does* with those feelings is a whole other matter.

If I'm very angry, then something causes me to be angry. A situation happened that prompted me to be angry, and therefore, my anger is valid. However, what I do with that anger can be allowed or not. The way that I deal with my anger can have negative consequences, so the behaviors can become bad, but the emotions never are.

If I'm angry at an individual because they hurt me or disappointed me, then I have a right to feel that anger. I don't have a right to punch them in the face!

One of the things that I challenge you as the reader is to not be so quick to place your own judgment on someone else's emotions. Don't be so quick to place judgment on someone else's experiences because they're not your own.

Listening with the goal of understanding—not responding—is a relationship game-changer.

This can manifest in endless ways. Say you lost a pet, and you're devastated by this loss because your pet has become an extension of you. They were your best friend, and they were the most cherished being in your entire world. Others may think that your devastation is an overreaction because they're "just an animal." You'd be pretty upset about this response because what they're not doing is validating your feelings about your loss.

In my experience, we're so notoriously bad about validating other people's emotions and experiences. We're so bad about allowing others to have their own thoughts, and this ties into so many realms.

One of the obvious platforms we see this manifest is in the realm of politics and how divided we can get in politics. Sometimes, it's okay to agree to disagree, especially when two people have very strong differing beliefs about the world.

We often think that when we have beliefs, when we have thoughts and feelings about things, if someone else's thoughts and feelings are different from ours, then they must be wrong. But that's not necessarily the case. Multiple beliefs can coexist.

Take religion as an example. There are so many religions and belief systems, and they can all coexist because one belief works for one person, and a directly opposing belief works as well for another person. Ultimately, they all become the "right" religions because they are right for the individual who believes them. It reminds me of a quote I saw at a vet's office: "Everyone thinks they have the best dog in the world, and everyone is right."

Anything that is outside the realm of solid facts, i.e., beliefs, feelings, values, etc., also falls outside the realm of solid right and wrong. When things in this realm are right, it's because it's *right for that individual.* This is the piece we keep missing. Even when you feel strongly about something because that is right for you, it doesn't mean that you get to say that the same thing is right for everyone else.

We also know that beliefs come from values, and this is also relevant in the realm of political differences. Some things are important to some people, and the opposite things are important to others because their values are different. Values don't exist in the realm of solid fact, and therefore, when someone has their values about something, those values are right for them.

Values can even coexist because they are not objective facts. Values are in the realm of subjectivity and individual perspective, and they stem from how we make sense of the world. They come from our learning and our experiences, as I discussed in an earlier chapter.

If I have certain values and beliefs about the world, formed from my experiences and creating my outlook on the world, then this is what I find important. Someone else may have had very different experiences, and therefore, they've formed very different values.

My goal is not to get into political debates. The point I want to make is more about the psychology behind where those differences come from and why differences can become so heated with anger and right and wrong. The reason why differences in values turn into such conflict is because of the inability to accept the fact that someone else has a different experience and allow that different experience to exist.

It makes me think of all the religious wars that stem from belief systems being wrongfully turned into facts. Now, some can believe in their faith so strongly that there is no alternative but for it to be a fact to them, but ultimately, it is still a belief system. Spiritually, in the end, we don't know what is real and not real until we're no longer around to share this knowledge!

All religions can coexist because, as mentioned before, they work for the believer. If someone feels very strongly about their religion and it becomes true for them, what often happens is that they place their truth onto others and feel like others need to believe the same thing they do. This is the opposite of validation.

Validation can allow two people from very different religions who feel very strongly about their own religion to come together and allow the other person to have their belief system. This is because they can acknowledge that even though their religion is the truth for them, it doesn't mean it's the truth for someone else. They can make peace with the fact that multiple different viewpoints exist. This is validation.

Disagreement doesn't require defensiveness, it requires curiosity.

Whenever we see what's going on in the world and we are exposed to news headlines, we immediately form opinions about what is real and what isn't. We have debates about what should be happening or why something is happening in the first place, but we also need to remind ourselves that whatever opinions we have about different situations, we can only make those opinions based on the factual knowledge we have and I'm willing to bet that most of the time this knowledge is very limited.

When we hear people making decisions that we don't agree with, we often immediately have an opinion about why that decision is wrong and what they should be doing instead. However, what we're not doing is working on understanding why that person is making that decision and why their decision was important to them. We often make no effort to understand their side of things and to work on understanding their values, even if they are different from our own.

In the end nobody is qualified to make decisions except for the individual themselves. Every single person who is not the person in question has an opinion about what the individual should be doing but this will always be an opinion based on their limited subjective perspective.

So now, I challenge you to hold back. Can you challenge yourself to see something from someone else's perspective and allow their experience to be valid even and especially when it differs from your own?

If you're in a relationship and you're reading this, I would challenge you to do the same thing with your partner. When you try to form judgments or opinions about your partner because they have a different way of seeing things, is there a way that your differences can coexist?

If you're in a relationship where your differing perspectives, values, and beliefs often conflict with each other, maybe you and your partner can begin to see things from each other's perspectives. There's an exercise I often give couples in counseling that can help with this.

When I have couples in for counseling, quite often, I see that the conflict between them stems from a belief turning into a fact; therefore, they are right, and the other is wrong. I see couples struggling to validate each other, and often, there isn't even the opportunity to explain their beliefs and viewpoints because the listening is not even present, and both parties are very quick to defend their viewpoint in the need to be "right."

When I see that this lack of validation has become a barrier, there's a particular exercise I ask them to engage in to practice working on understanding each other's viewpoints more. First, it's always important to start small because applying this exercise to bigger and heavier topics can lead to conflict.

I ask the couple to find something somewhat small that they don't agree on, for example, a movie. Maybe one-half of the couple loves a particular movie, and the other doesn't like it at all. A movie is usually neutral ground because we can easily accept the fact that people like different genres. We often don't have an issue with people having different opinions about movies.

When the couple has found a movie that they disagree on and have a very different opinion on, I'll ask the couple to talk about the movie. The person who is talking about the movie has to talk about why they do or don't like the movie. The person who is listening has to listen with a goal in mind. The goal is not to disagree and share why their opinion is different. No, the person who is listening has to place an emphasis on trying to understand why the other person has their perspective.

So when the person who talks about the movie explains why they like the movie, maybe they explain that it's because the movie is a story about redemption, or maybe it's a movie not to be taken seriously and it's precisely the silliness that they like. Or maybe they like a particular actor, or maybe it highlights an issue they feel passionate about. The listener has the job to work on understanding why that movie is liked by their partner.

Then I get the couple to switch roles, and now the other half has the opportunity to say why they don't like the movie. Maybe they don't like the genre, or they read the book first, and the movie doesn't do it justice. And their other half works on understanding that perspective.

Of course, in an exercise like this, it's important for the person who is sharing what they didn't like about the movie to not turn their opinion into a bitchfest, as this will raise defensiveness. Their goal is to explain in a way that they are sharing where they're coming from. Or maybe they can share a movie that they liked that their partner didn't and then discuss why they liked that particular movie.

The point is the listener has the task to work on understanding the other person. It's almost like they are given the challenge to see if they can understand why the other person has their perspective. The focus, the goal, is not about who is right or wrong, or who speaks the loudest wins. All of that becomes irrelevant. The focus is on working on understanding a new perspective.

Taking this exercise a step further, maybe this approach can be applied more in everyday life also. When someone is talking about something, whether it's a story about something that happened to them or they're sharing an opinion about something, instead of forming an opinion about them in a critical or judgmental way, maybe work on reframing your approach and see if you can work on understanding where that person is coming from.

Maybe instead of forming opinions yourself, you can work on telling yourself why their opinion is valid. When you see people making decisions in the news, instead of dismissing these decisions immediately, see if you can work to understand why they came to those decisions.

Put yourself in the other person's shoes and work on seeing things through their lens. Work on understanding why their decisions were important to them, even if they don't make sense to you. I think we need to do more of this.

When someone comes to you with different opinions, listen first. Validate first.

One example of working on understanding another's perspective, an example I use in my counseling practice, is that if someone tells a joke and they think it's funny, but you're offended by that joke, then your feelings are valid. If you tell that person that you know they think the joke is funny but you find it offensive and you tell them why, one classic reaction would be to get defensive or to tell the offended person they're overreacting or so. But what they're not doing is validating the fact that they are offended by something they didn't find funny.

What happens when validation is present is that the person acknowledges that they offended someone without realizing it. That doesn't mean that they now also have to think that the joke wasn't funny. It means that they acknowledge that somebody had a different feeling about something, and they were allowed to have this feeling because it's valid for them.

A by-product of working to develop a greater understanding of others and their beliefs is an increase in your compassion toward others. One of the benefits of increasing compassion is you reduce your own feelings of frustration and intolerance of others, making this a step toward a more peaceful coexistence.

11

MINDFULNESS

Mindfulness is a topic I frequently discuss with my clients. We often hear that we should practice it, and we hear that practicing mindfulness is going to help our lives, but I believe it's become more like one of those wellness/self-help practices we should be doing that healthy people do every day.

We know that mindfulness is in the realm of wellness, but how many people have actually explored the benefits of it and how exactly it contributes to wellness? We know that mindfulness is a healthy practice, but do we know why? How can applying it have a beneficial impact on our lives? What changes take place in our lives when we practice mindfulness?

First, we need to explore what mindfulness actually is. What does it even mean to practice mindfulness? Then, we can explore how to incorporate the process into our lives.

Let's begin by talking about mindfulness and meditation. These are two different things, and it seems like these are often compared or used interchangeably.

Mindfulness is the practice of focusing your mind only on one thing at a time. It's about whatever it is that you're doing at any given moment; that is where your full attention goes. This is not about emptying your mind but about whatever it is that you're doing; then, that's the only thing that you're doing.

With mindfulness, you are fully present in every moment. You're fully present with every action you take. If you're having a conversation with someone, be present in the conversation. If you're paying attention to your phone or thinking about all the things you still need to do that day, then you're not being present in your conversation, and you're not practicing mindfulness.

When you do the dishes at home, you could be doing the dishes and at the same time thinking about how much you hate doing the dishes and about all the things you wish you were doing instead of doing the dishes. However, mindfully doing the dishes is about being fully present with the dishes.

Meditation is the activity of practicing mindfulness. Meditation is an action, whereas mindfulness is a state of being.

Doing the dishes mindfully is about taking the judgment out of doing the dishes, e.g., ugh, doing dishes sucks, I don't want to be doing this, etc., and when you take these thoughts out of your mind, then doing the dishes just is. The dishes no longer become a bad thing or a good thing; it just is.

In this way, you can allow yourself to become fully present in doing the dishes, and now your focus shifts from negative thoughts to maybe the temperature of the water, feeling the soapy texture on your hands, and you're present in the activity. You get on with doing the dishes without having all the emotional attachment of how much you hate it and how much you wish you weren't doing the dishes right now. It just is.

Mindfulness is the idea that whatever you're doing at any given moment, that's the only thing that you're doing. The beauty of it is that it's something we can do no matter where we are. We don't have to take time out of our day to practice the process because, by default, practice is in the things we're already doing.

Be present while watching a movie. Don't watch TV... and read... and do homework... and browse the internet. Focus on each at a time.

You don't have to take time out of your schedule to practice mindfulness. This is incorporated into the things you're already doing. It's that you're now more present in those things.

The thing that separates mindfulness from meditation is that meditation is the activity of practicing mindfulness. Meditation is an action, whereas mindfulness is a state of being. Meditation is a separate activity that involves practicing mindfulness.

Because meditation is an activity, you do set time aside to practice this, and in meditation, you practice focusing on only one thing, thereby practicing mindfulness during meditation. A lot of times, the mindfulness practice of focusing on only one thing at the moment within meditation is focusing on the breath.

When you focus solely on your breathing, you're simply being aware of your breathing. All of your attention and focus is on your breathing. What does it feel like? Can you feel the air move in and out of you? Can you feel the warm exhale of your breath?

Meditation, therefore, is the practice of mindfulness, and the one thing to direct your attention to during the activity of meditation is the breath.

One thing I can tell you about the practice is that it can be extremely difficult. Our minds have a tendency to be all over the place. In Buddhism, this is called the "Monkey Mind." This monkey tends to jump from branch to branch, and this is exactly what happens with our thoughts.

If we set an intention to practice mindfulness, we can do this by tidying the house and focusing on tidying the house. Well, you might have put one thing away, and you might already be thinking about what you're having for dinner tonight, what work looks like tomorrow, etc. Then you forget to practice it, and maybe only every now and then you remember that you intended to practice it in the first place!

The practice is a process, and it's one of those that you have to build up slowly, like any good habit. When I wrote about what happens in your brain when neurons that fire together wire together, the practice of mindfulness is a similar thing.

In the beginning, you might have to work continuously through constant repetition to focus your mind on one thing because our minds are incredibly distracted. But I do know that this process will get easier over time because what you're essentially doing is the same as building muscle.

As we know, when you build muscle, you're building strength over time. With muscle strength, heavier weights become easier, and you may be able to lift weights that you couldn't a year before. Mindfulness works the same way.

You might literally be able to hold your attention for only five seconds on something, but with continued practice, you may find that you can hold your attention for a little longer and then a bit longer still.

A good place to start is wherever you're at now. You identify your starting place, and for some people, this may be a few seconds of attention or a few minutes. If this is the case, start there. When you get distracted, gently bring your focus back to mindfulness.

Another thing I have observed a lot in my practice and also in the world, in general, is how distracted we all are. Life, society, and especially social media are all catered toward distractibility. We struggle to focus for long periods due to constant distractions in society, which cater to shorter attention spans.

Multi-tasking is mostly perceived as a desirable ability and people boast about being very good at multi-tasking. But actually, multitasking is a horrible habit to get into. If you watch regular TV, you can get into a show, and you have your attention on it, and a few minutes later, there are commercials. Social media is designed to shorten our attention more and more, with condensed versions of communication, be it through text or video.

Our minds are constantly being pulled in many directions, and this is a very common thing. If there's a very short article about something, say a magazine article, very rarely do people sit and read the entire thing because we don't have the attention span for it. We might start reading the article, and we may make it through the first few paragraphs, but we're usually very bad at following through and reading the entire thing. This is because we're becoming so much more distracted.

The senses are always in-the-moment experiences.
Use them to bring yourself back to now.

The thing that gets us away from being distracted like that is the practice of mindfulness. If you plan on reading an article, sit with the article and read the whole thing. If you have to do homework or there's a project you're working on, make time for that and sit with it.

One of the tendencies that we have is to try to keep thoughts in our minds to keep ourselves from forgetting them. This is also another reason why we keep ourselves distracted, e.g., we remember we need to do something like make a phone call, and then we try to keep this thing in our minds so that we won't forget about it, but it also diminishes our ability to focus and be present with whatever it is we're doing.

The easiest way to counter this is by writing it down. As soon as the thought pops into your mind of something you need to do, e.g., a phone call you need to make, write it down. That way, you can let go of the thought, and you can continue focusing on whatever it is you're doing because now you don't have to actively try and remember this thing.

This way, you can build this habit from here; getting in the habit of writing things down or making a notation of them as they come up will allow more mental space to practice mindfulness.

Whereas meditation is an intended activity, mindfulness doesn't take any extra time out of your schedule. You can still continue with your usual routine, and nothing about that has to change. You simply add mindfulness to your existing routine.

Another reason we're so forgetful, e.g., we put our keys down and then we can't find them anywhere (sound familiar?), is because we need attention for memory recall. If we don't pay attention to something, our brains cannot store that information. If you mindlessly put your keys down on the table while you're focusing on something else, your brain has not had an opportunity to store that information in your memory, and so, of course, you can't find your keys! There is no memory recall of where you put your keys because there was no attention there.

This is one of the reasons why mindfulness can help with focus, concentration, and memory, because it helps you pay attention to your actions, and there's more room for those actions to be stored into your memory.

If you're practicing mindfulness and you put your keys away, or you are mindfully present when you put your keys on the table, then you're paying attention to that, so now this action can be entered into your memory. Now, when you need to find your keys, you know exactly where they are.

We do this all the time. We walk into a room and then forget what we walked into the room for. We look for a pen, knowing that we had the pen but now we can't find it. Small occurrences like this happen all the time and it's because we're so distracted. Mindfulness is a practice that can counter this.

There are so many benefits of mindfulness. Mindfulness can help reduce anxiety because mindfulness puts us in the present moment.

What's in the past is not changeable, and we can mull over the shoulda/woulda/coulda's, but in the end, what's done is done. We'll never be able to change the past. Mindfulness can get us out of that anxiety and out of our regrets, out of our self-judgments and negative self-talk because when we apply mindfulness, we redirect our minds back to the here and now.

When we place our focus back on the here and now, we acknowledge what is real in this very moment, and there is less room in our minds to focus on the past when it's the here and now that is real in-the-moment.

The same goes for anxieties based on the future. A lot of anxieties stem from future worry, i.e., the what-ifs. Our minds are amazing at coming up with all these hypotheticals about the future, and we can spend an endless amount of time worrying about what if this, what if that, and how is this future thing going to work out, etc. When you apply mindfulness and bring yourself back to the present moment, you focus on what is real right now.

Mindfulness makes you identify what is real in-the-moment, and you can focus on what you can do in-the-moment to make your future go as well as possible. For example, if you have something coming up in the future that causes some anxiety, whether it's a public speaking event or a project that you're working on, or you have to do something you've never done before, the tendency would be to engage in future worrying about these scenarios.

You may experience a lot of worry thoughts in the realm of performance, success, failure, etc. However, all these types of worry are all future-oriented. When you bring yourself back to the present moment and ask yourself what you can do to make the outcome as successful as possible, you're focusing on the present.

Another thing that mindfulness does is that it acknowledges what is real in the here and now. If you have something coming up in the future that increases anxiety, like public speaking or performing, then thinking about this can cause anxiety and worry thoughts. However, when you apply mindfulness, you can acknowledge that right now, in this moment, this event is not happening.

At this very moment, this future event is not real. Right now, at that very moment, you could be at your desk with the project in front of you, and that's what you're focusing on. Because the event you're worrying about is not real in the present, why go through the anxiety unnecessarily?

Applying mindfulness can reduce your anxiety in that moment because you're recognizing that the object of your anxiety is not happening.

If you have trouble with practicing mindfulness or even have trouble bringing yourself back to the here and now, one practice that can help with this is getting your senses engaged. The senses are always in-the-moment experiences.

When you hear things, you don't hear something that happened ten minutes ago. You don't hear things that are going to happen ten minutes from now. Everything that you hear is always right now. The senses are always simply happening in the present.

In any given moment, with everything you see, you're seeing what's in front of you right now. You're not seeing things that happened yesterday or will happen tomorrow. Everything that your vision is focused on is always here and now.

The same thing goes for touch. What is it that you can feel? You can feel your clothes on your skin or the room temperature. You can feel the warmth of a cup of coffee as you drink it. Those are all sensations that you only feel in the present. Not yesterday or tomorrow, but only now.

When you engage all your senses and bring your focus back to the here and now, a good practice is to go through all the senses one by one and ask yourself: What can I see right now? What can I hear? What taste is still in my mouth? This is one way that can get you back to center.

This can also be used as a grounding skill for high anxiety. By focusing on the senses, you're effectively telling your brain to identify that whatever threat it's responding to is not real, and it can allow your body to move back from stress response to relaxation response.

Reducing anxiety is one of the major advantages of mindfulness. Practicing mindfulness no longer remains a concept but a very real applicable practice to manage mental health symptoms. It can help reframe negative and critical thoughts because you're identifying the difference between what is real and what is thought.

When you tell yourself that you're such a failure or that you feel worthless, then you can ask yourself what you are doing right now in this moment. Maybe you're listening to this book while you're driving, and right at that moment, behind the wheel, there's no evidence, absolutely nothing to suggest that you're any of those things.

You just are. Everything simply becomes. It just is. Things don't become right or wrong, bad or good, they just are. Mindfulness can help take the judgment out of situations, and it allows you to see situations as being. Situations become not necessarily negative; they simply are.

The thing that makes something good or bad is always the judgment we attach to it. If you get in your head that your presentation is going to be a disaster because of all the anxiety you experience about it, then this becomes a horrible and negative thing. But if you bring yourself back to center and recognize that the presentation just is, and while you present, you're talking to different individuals then that just is. It's not good or bad or horrible, it just is.

12
SELF-TALK

In this chapter, I want to talk a bit about the language we use and what we tell ourselves. I will be discussing how to change the experience we have about things. The topic of words and self-talk and the beliefs we hold about ourselves is such a broad subject that this subject could be a book in itself. However, I want to talk about more specific things in the realm of self-talk.

One thing I experience a lot with clients is that they have critical thoughts and judgments about their own past actions, restrictions they have placed on themselves, expectations they have set, and negative self-talk that goes along with all of this.

It's good to have goals, have high expectations of yourself, want to move forward in life and aim high. These are all positive things. The thing that makes it not positive, or the factor that can make these very unhealthy, is what you're telling yourself about the situation if you don't quite accomplish what you set out to do.

For example, if you strive to eat healthy and take better care of yourself, you may tell yourself you're going to eat all the right foods. You've read all about it, and you know what you need to do. So this is your new goal, and all day you do well but then in the evening you snack on unhealthy foods because maybe you're stressed, or you're hungry. So now you're struggling because as soon as you create restrictions for yourself, guess what you want now? Everything that you've restricted!

When you eat all the unhealthy snacks, initially, it may taste good, but as you eat more, you gradually feel worse and worse about yourself. Then you begin to tell yourself that you shouldn't be eating these snacks, that you're lazy, that you're a failure for not even making it through one day of healthy eating, you can never follow through with anything, it's always going to be like this, etc., etc., etc.

The next day, you wake up, and you feel guilty and horrible about it. You criticize your lack of control, and you highlight your failures.

The thing that makes something healthier or not is often your approach to it. Eating ice cream or different snacks is in itself not a bad thing. But what are you telling yourself about when you eat those things? Are you approaching it by telling yourself you shouldn't be doing it, or can you get to a place where you feel good that night, you're going to watch a good movie, have a good evening, and enjoy some snacks? Then, when you have those snacks, you can enjoy them guilt-free.

You're still eating the same foods but the language you use on yourself and the things you tell yourself about your actions, that's the thing that makes this action emotionally healthy or not.

When you're using negative language on yourself that's restrictive, perfectionistic, or expects way too much from yourself, then you're setting yourself up for all these negative feelings, and then it becomes a negative thing in your life. It now becomes an obligation or something that you're chained to, and you're now restricted in so many ways.

It's all about paying attention to the language. For example, if you set out to lose ten pounds this month, and then you stand on the scale at the end of the month, and you've lost three pounds, you may instantly begin with negative self-talk, telling yourself you didn't reach your goal, you only lost three pounds and not ten, at this rate you'll never get to your goal, what's the point in even trying?

With this mindset, everything about weight loss and everything about taking better care of yourself has become this negative thing in your mind and all these negative emotions are going to be attached to it, which is going to reflect in how you feel about yourself. This, in turn, creates a cycle of feeling worse about yourself. Because of this, you don't want to take care of yourself as much, so you might engage in habits that are worse for you, which makes you feel worse about yourself and on and on and on.

However, if you stand on the scale and you've lost three pounds instead of ten, what is the language you're using on yourself about this? Can you say to yourself wow, I lost three pounds! That's progress! That's better than it was a month ago! You can tell yourself that you didn't lose as much as you wanted to this month, so you'll keep working at it. Or you may revise your monthly goal to make it more realistic for yourself.

You could maybe recognize other ways in which your health is improving, for example, by telling yourself that even though you didn't lose the weight you intended to, you still ate healthier and took better care of yourself and that in itself is a good thing. You could recognize that you felt better because of eating healthier and that's a win.

So many times, we create way too many restrictions on ourselves, especially in the realm of self-care and nutrition. We tell ourselves that we need to eat all the right things and we need to have a good breakfast, drink lots of water, limit our fat intake, limit this and limit that. Again, these limits may be a good thing, and they may be what are necessary to reach your goal, however, when you do have one of the things that were supposed to be restricted, now there's guilt attached.

Now you feel bad about yourself because you did something that you told yourself you weren't supposed to do.

This is so incredibly toxic because you're creating all these negative experiences for yourself when it doesn't have to be this way. When you go to a restaurant, and you have dessert, there's a huge difference between telling yourself you know you shouldn't have this dessert, but you're going to have it anyway, and oh no, you're going to put weight back on, you failed in your diet because you had dessert. Or you can approach it with more positive self-talk, such as you've been feeling good about yourself, you've worked hard to stay healthy, and you're going to enjoy and savor the taste of this dessert.

You're eating the same dessert, but you're giving yourself a whole different experience with it. Research even showed that people who had guilt and negative feelings associated with food actually lost less weight.[1]

This concept is something I talk about frequently with my clients. We acknowledge the situation and then explore the language they are using on themselves about the situation.

One approach I like to make it a little easier is to turn yourself into an objective observer. This is also taking the approach that everything is neutral. Everything that happens in life just is. It's what we tell ourselves about the situation and the language we use on ourselves that makes something good or bad.

Many times we'll tell ourselves that we'll feel better about ourselves and we'll be happy when we reach a certain goal, be it weight or something else. But is it possible to be a little heavier and at the same time feel good about yourself? Of course, it is.

Some may believe that this will stop you from taking better care of yourself because you become complacent when you feel good about yourself already, but this is not the case. I've had many clients who believe that they will stop aiming for their goals if they become happier now and, therefore, don't allow themselves to be happier until they reach their goals. However, you can be happy now and still strive for better.

Say, for example, you're thirty pounds overweight, then you may tell yourself you need to lose the thirty pounds and when you do, you'll feel much better about yourself. When you lose those thirty pounds,

---

1. Kuijer R, Boyce J. Chocolate Cake: Guilt or Celebration? Associations with Healthy Eating Attitudes, Perceived Behavioural Control, Intentions and Weight-loss. Appetite. 2013.

you'll feel more active and energized, and you'll feel healthier and more confident. That in itself is a great goal. However, what are you telling yourself about where you're at right now? Are you telling yourself that because you're currently overweight, you're a slob, and you're ashamed of yourself? Are you telling yourself that you hate yourself and the way you look? Are you telling yourself that you'll feel good about yourself only when you've lost the weight?

Could you feel good about yourself now? You have some goals to work on, like losing weight, because you know you'll feel healthier and more energized. But you also love yourself right now. Can you tell yourself now that you feel good about yourself now because the way you are right now, that just is?

And if the way you are right now just is, why would you want to hide that? This is you; take it or leave it. The way you are right now is neutral, and it's all the judgment and criticism you are placing on your situation that makes it a negative situation.

You can still feel good about yourself because this is who you are right now, and at the same time, you can continue working on weight loss and feeling healthier because you know you'll feel even better.

The goals haven't changed. You haven't become complacent and haven't stopped working on reaching your goals. When you reframe the language and allow yourself to feel good about yourself now, it doesn't stop you from moving forward. You can still work on accomplishing your goals in the exact same way as someone who doesn't feel good about themselves.

You might actually be more successful because your whole approach to health changes. Your whole approach to health and foods and all of that changes because when you feel good about yourself today, you might naturally want to take better care of yourself because you already like who you are right now.

Now, if you do enjoy a treat or a dessert, or have a drink with friends, or you go through a fast-food drive thru, guess what? You're not going to feel guilty about it because you know that you're focusing primarily on health, you know you feel good about yourself, and you know that, for the most part, you're doing well, so one deviation does not make you a failure.

It doesn't mean that you're undoing all the work you've done so far and that all your work has been a waste of time. It means that you've taken all those restrictions away, and you're focusing on health.

One of the restrictions we often place on ourselves is timelines. We tell ourselves that we want to be a certain weight by our birthday, the summer, or another specific date. We set timelines, and quite often, the closer we get to those timelines, the harder it becomes. Now we're under pressure.

Now our goals have changed from losing one pound a week to needing to lose two pounds a week. We tell ourselves that we now need to step up our game, and now we become even more restrictive. The language we use on ourselves becomes even more negative. However, when we take away those restrictions, we can allow ourselves to continue working on our goals.

Without these unnecessary pressures and increased restrictions, we can allow ourselves to continue focusing on health, and as long as today is the same or better than yesterday, we will inevitably get to our goal.

I want to emphasize that setting timelines for goals is not in itself a bad thing. Quite often, we need to work with timelines to accomplish goals. The point that is important here is that sometimes, the timelines we place on ourselves are unnecessary, and they add restrictions. They add to our negative self-talk; they add pressure and ultimately end up working against us.

Our self-talk becomes important because we can use such restrictive language on ourselves. We have the potential to be incredibly cruel and harsh toward ourselves, telling ourselves that we're a complete failure if we don't reach a certain goal by a certain date.

If you're able to take away the unnecessary restrictions and focus on your goals, without adding negative self-talk to your current situation, then you begin to focus more on the positive outcomes of your goals. You focus more on how your goals will enhance your life even more.

The reframe also needs to start from an emotional place rather than a physical place. What often doesn't work is when we tell ourselves that we're going to feel better emotionally and psychologically when we feel better physically or when we've accomplished our goal. What works better is that we can engage in better physical health when we start with our emotions.

When you start to feel better about yourself, and you reframe the self-talk and turn that negative language about yourself into something healthier, then physical health may naturally follow because you're freed up from all these restrictions, and you naturally want to make healthier choices.

If you place ten different toys in front of a child, and you tell them that they aren't allowed to play with one of them, guess which one they're going to want to play with? Exactly.

Adults work the same way. As soon as something becomes a restriction, we want it more. When we restrict something, it becomes a lack in our lives, and when something is a lack, it becomes a stress because we know we'll never be able to have it again. Food is, of course, the primary example. It becomes this unhealthy thing, and once we've restricted a food, it's often the one thing we want, and now we end up eating too much of it.

Maybe this stems partly from our survival instinct. When we know that something is gone from our lives, we want to hoard as much of it as we can, but if we know that something is always going to be there, then the urgency of having this thing now is gone because we know we can have it at any time.

If you want to enjoy a burger at a fast-food chain, the likelihood is that it's always going to be there. It's easier to say no to the burger today and make healthier choices because you know that if you wanted to, you could have it tomorrow. But if we're told that the fast-food chain is going away, then I can guarantee that the lines for those same burgers will be endless.

This same thing happened in the spring of 2020 when COVID-19 hit. In England, McDonald's announced they were shutting down for a while. It was the last day that they were open, and the lines outside McDonald's restaurants were ridiculous.

People knew they were going to be restricted for a while, not even permanently. They now had a greater urgency to want those burgers today!

This is how our brains are wired. When you take away restriction and focus on health, you can reframe from restriction to knowing you want to be healthier, so you focus instead on healthier choices. This way, you're not necessarily restricting yourself in any way. You may choose not to have something today, but you're also not telling yourself you can never have it. This lack of restriction makes it easier for you to feel good about your choices because those choices are not forced.

This is another aspect that creates resistance. When you tell yourself you have to eat something in particular because you're on a certain diet and they only allow certain types of foods, those foods that you have to eat stop being as enjoyable because it's a forced choice. However, by reframing your focus back on health and wanting to take better care of yourself, and as a result, you choose to eat healthier foods. That choice was more natural, and you will enjoy those foods more.

As you see, there are so many by-products to paying attention to the language we use on ourselves. The same applies to individuals who have perfectionist tendencies.

Perfectionists tend to have very high goals for themselves. They set very high expectations of themselves. That in itself is not a bad thing. People who do amazing things in the world and accomplish great things wouldn't have done so if they didn't have these high expectations of themselves.

What I'm asking you is, what are you telling yourself when you don't quite meet those expectations?

For example, you tell yourself that your goal is to be able to run a marathon; you work hard, train hard, and then you sign up for a marathon. Then, at mile twenty-three, you cramp up, your body gives up, and you're not able to finish.

The factor that becomes very important here is the language you use on yourself. Are you telling yourself you're a complete failure because you didn't complete the marathon? Are you telling yourself that all your hard work was for nothing because you weren't able to complete and get your finisher's medal? Are you telling yourself that this was a big waste of time? Are you now doubting that you'll be able to accomplish anything you set your mind to?

Or do you tell yourself, "Holy crap, I ran twenty-three miles!" Maybe a few years before you didn't even think you could run a 5k, and here you are, running twenty-three miles! Do you see the wonder in that? Are you telling yourself that running twenty-three miles is an amazing accomplishment? Are you reminding yourself that you did the best that you could, and you feel good about giving it your all?

You could even remind yourself that you dared to train for such a huge endeavor that you didn't think you'd ever sign up for or train for. You could remind yourself that even though you didn't get to the finish line, you signed up and trained for it! You did more than most people!

The thing is, the outcome is the same. You ran twenty-three miles instead of 26.2 and couldn't go any further. The outcome of your situation hasn't changed. The thing that makes all the difference in how you feel and what you take away from the situation is the story you're telling yourself about it. It's all about the language you use on yourself—the narrative changes with the self-talk.

It's the story you tell yourself that will ultimately change the whole experience that you have about the situation. And it doesn't mean at all that you won't ever run a marathon ever again. Maybe you'll even go back and think about the things you could've done better. Maybe you identified that you pushed yourself too hard at the start line. Maybe you identify that you didn't eat properly in the days leading up to the race. After your experience and your cognitive reframe, you can now start to evaluate the things you can improve on. The important thing is the language.

This is a recurring conversation I have with a lot of my clients. When it comes to working on goals and having goals and expectations, this is a positive thing because it drives us to move forward in life and improve our lives. But pay attention to your language. Pay attention to the narrative when you don't meet your expectations.

As I mentioned earlier, feeling good about where you are now is not the same as complacency. For example, if you tell yourself that you're okay with accomplishing running twenty-three miles instead of twenty-six, does that make you not want to sign up for a marathon to see if you can make it to twenty-six miles? Of course not! If anything, I'm willing to bet that you'd be even more motivated.

When you change the language, and you're no longer using all the negative, critical, and judgmental language on yourself for not accomplishing your end goals, you're sparing yourself from a negative emotional experience, and you're being kinder and more compassionate toward yourself, while at the same time continuing to work on furthering those goals.

Part of the reframing from negative self-talk to positive self-talk is about being more compassionate toward yourself. You're being kinder to yourself, and this is not the same as complacency. It's not the same as settling for less. If anything, using a positive reframe will allow you to reach your goals more effectively because you take away many of the restrictions you've unnecessarily placed on yourself.

13
NOTHING IS PERSONAL

Another recurring conversation in my counseling sessions is the theme of taking things personally. This concept is about the fact that nothing is ever personal, but this is a very difficult concept to grasp because a lot of things feel very personal.

When someone directs hurtful words at you while looking at you, it feels very personal. But even then, nothing is truly personal. This is what I want to talk about.

Anything that anyone ever says or does is an accumulation of their experiences and their perspective in that given moment, and this is what is being expressed in that moment. Everyone is so vastly different and unique because everyone comes from their own unique life experiences. Everyone is constantly learning and discovering their values, beliefs, etc.

Everyone ultimately has a different perspective on every experience, and there are so many factors that cause someone to have their outlook at any given moment in time.

> **Two people can see the same thing and form completely different opinions, based on what's inside them, not what's in front of them.**

Some of the factors that contribute to someone's perspective include their learning, their upbringing, their social experiences, their education, their family life, the role-modeling they've received, their peers, influences from general people, relationships, etc.

Even how someone feels in any given moment, e.g., current emotions, current stress levels, their current self-care, e.g., hunger or fatigue, contributes to someone's state of being in-the-moment. These momentary factors can also influence a person's perspective at any time.

When someone engages in a behavior, no matter what it is, they are responding to something based on everything that they know at that moment in time. The behavior comes from their perspective of the situation.

If someone is responding to you, then they are responding based on what their understanding is of what you said or did. For example, if you say something and someone else doesn't hear it correctly, so it comes across as offensive, then that individual is going to become offended and may respond defensively. When the misinterpretation is cleared up, then that individual's response may change significantly.

The reason the individual was offended by what you said was not because of what you said, but because of their perspective about what you said. Everyone's experiences in their lifetime are simply an accumulation of their subjective experiences.

For example, there is research on eyewitness testimony, and sometimes, multiple different people are experiencing and witnessing the same event. However, many of those individuals are going to report something different based on their subjective experience of the incident because of how they looked at the situation.

Everyone sees different things in their environment based on their preferences and experiences. You could have ten different people looking at the same thing, and all of them could pick up on something different based on what they've homed in on. Different things are going to jump out to different people because all ten people are uniquely different.

When people respond in certain ways, that is more a reflection of them than it is of anybody else, because they are responding based on their perspective. You can have someone who, for example, works in retail, new and nervous, and then they receive a difficult customer who is mean and has unrealistic expectations.

The retail worker might take the interaction personally. They could feel they didn't do a good job because of the criticism, leaving them feeling bad about the customer's harsh feedback.

However, the behavior of that customer is more a reflection of that customer than it is of the retail worker. This is because the retail worker can change absolutely nothing about the way they work, and a different customer could come in and treat that retail worker very well. The nice customer could tell the retail worker that they've worked retail before; they understand it can get overwhelming, most especially when you're new, and they may show this retail worker more patience and grace.

Nothing about what the retail worker did was any different. However, the response was different because the response was a reflection of the customer, not the retail worker.

When someone is negative toward you, angry, and hurtful, that says a whole lot more about that individual than it does about you. Unfortunately, we often don't understand this, especially as kids. As adults, we can learn to grasp this concept that nothing is ever personal, especially when people are critical or judgmental of us and our choices. Instead of becoming self-conscious because of the criticisms and judgments of others, we can learn that their judgment is a reflection of them and not you.

When you understand that everything is shaped by individual perspectives, you understand that criticism, like disapproval of your style of dress, stems from others not liking it because it doesn't fit in with what *they* would wear. It doesn't fit in with *their* style and what *they* like. It doesn't mean that what you're wearing is wrong or ugly, simply because it's what you like. It feels right for you.

This is exactly why there are so many styles of things, different genres of movies and music, different styles of clothing, different hairstyles, different types of cars, different sports, and different types of recreational activities. There are so many types of things that people do because it's all based on individual preferences.

Some people like country music, and some people hate country music. That doesn't mean that anyone is wrong; it means that that experience, that preference, is right for them. This also applies to judgments and criticisms. When you take something personally, then you're thinking that someone else's opinion relates to you, but it doesn't.

If someone criticizes the way you dress, you may be hurt by that, but hopefully, you're also able to recognize that this is their opinion, their perspective about it, and allow that perspective. That doesn't mean that it's true for you. They may wonder what you were thinking when you chose your outfit, but you are wearing it because it feels right for you.

Criticism is often a mirror, not a spotlight.

When someone chooses to be nice or mean to someone else, it says a lot more about them as an individual. If someone instantly judges another person because of having a different style, then that instant criticism says something about them as a person. If someone is nice and respectful, they may look at someone else with a different clothing style, and they may tell themselves that they wouldn't suit that style of clothing, but likely the wording and the judgment about the other person's style wouldn't necessarily be negative.

Negative and judgmental individuals are a lot quicker to jump to criticisms of others, but it's a reflection of them as negative or judgmental individuals, not on you, who is on the receiving end of the judgments.

Maybe that need to criticize others indicates something in them, whether it's an insecurity or a lack in some way. The point is that when someone is mean or hurtful, even then, it's still not personal because that behavior says a lot more about them as an individual than it does you.

Even though nothing is ever personal, what I'm not saying is that it's not hurtful. Words and actions are particularly impactful with children. A lot of the lasting impact of judgments and criticism begins in childhood. The negative core beliefs children form from judgments and criticisms during childhood impact their self-worth, which in turn influences their behaviors and responses.

As adults, we can recognize that we can protect ourselves from getting hurt by recognizing that things are not personal. Even with the bully in the playground, it's not personal. It can feel extremely personal, but it's not. This doesn't excuse their behavior by any means; it can help explain their behavior, but it still doesn't excuse their behavior.

The bully in the playground could be bullying because, at home, they're being bullied by their parents or siblings, and they may feel like they have no control over their life. They may feel like the only way they can assert any kind of control in their life is by controlling others. Or maybe they've been so hurt in their life that the only way they know to protect themselves is to be angry and to show aggressive behaviors, because it keeps everyone at a distance. It becomes a protection because if you keep people at a distance, they can't hurt you.

That bully's behavior says a lot more about them than it does about the people they are bullying. As adults, we can understand this, but once again, it doesn't excuse that behavior.

Being able to grasp that people's behaviors and responses say a lot more about them than it does about you makes it easier not to take it on. It's easier not to take things personally when you know someone is engaging in negative behaviors, whether it be through words or actions; then, it's not a reflection of you but a reflection of them. You happen to be the outlet.

Another important thing to add when I talk about this is that it's still important to protect yourself against negative behaviors. If someone is being hurtful toward you, then you can recognize that it's not personal and that hurtful behavior is a result of what that individual is going through or how they're feeling in that moment. However, it doesn't make that behavior okay, and it doesn't mean that you have to put up with it because you recognize that it's not about you.

Of course, it's appropriate to protect yourself against negative behaviors, to place boundaries, and not to allow or accept certain negative things in your life.

What I'm not saying is that when you recognize that others are being verbally or physically hurtful toward you, you allow and accept this behavior into your life. I'm not saying that you should continue to accept this negative behavior in your life because it doesn't reflect on you, anyway.

What I am saying is that you don't have to internalize the behaviors and judgments of others. You don't have to take their belief on and let someone else's judgment and perspective about you become a belief about yourself. You don't have to change your self-value based on someone else's perspective or an opinion that someone else has about you because, ultimately, their opinion is their stuff, not yours.

The only person who can know you is you. You're the only person who has gone through your experiences. You're the only person who has felt your feelings and interpreted your experiences. All the experiences, feelings, thoughts, memories, etc., that you've experienced in your life are only uniquely your experiences, and all of these influence how you will respond at any moment in time. It's all this learning and experiencing combined that allows you to make any decision at any moment in time.

The only person who can be a judge of your thoughts, feelings, and experiences is you.

Everyone else can have their opinions about different things, but it's never personal. Nothing is ever personal. Even when a behavior is directed at you, it's still not personal.

Two separate people could be looking at the same thing, e.g., a cyclist on the road, and one individual thinks, wow, that's cool, that cyclist is getting exercise, and they're taking care of their health, they're doing their part for the environment, and good for them. The other person could be looking at the same cyclist and think damn, cyclist, get off the road.

The cyclist is not doing anything different, but the opinions toward that cyclist are very different because they reflect the opinions of those individuals, not the cyclist.

This happens on so many levels in life. Whatever criticisms or judgments you hold about things in the world, these will come out in your perspective of others, and this always says a lot more about your perspective, not the person you are judging or criticizing. In the end, who are we to criticize or judge anyone?

The concept of not taking things personally takes place a lot in the realm of counseling because a lot of hurt and pain are attached to experiences. The impact of other people's behaviors and words on us is a whole separate topic. Because something isn't personal does not mean that we're not impacted by it.

As I mentioned earlier, as children, we're very much impacted by the words and actions of others. Not everyone knows that nothing is ever personal, especially children. Some people go a lifetime and still internalize the actions and words of others.

Now, I challenge you, the reader, to take more responsibility for the things you say to other people, especially your criticisms and judgments toward others. If you recognize that you tend to be critical or judgmental of others, then I challenge you to take a look at yourself, because when you're criticizing someone else, it's more a reflection of you. It doesn't say much about the individual you're criticizing because they are allowed their style and expression. They're allowed their behaviors, as long as they're not hurting anyone else, of course.

When you notice that you tend to react negatively toward an individual, I challenge you to look inward and to ask yourself what that criticism is reflecting in you. When you place judgment on someone else, what is it saying about you?

For anyone who wants to understand more about truly grasping this concept that nothing is personal, I highly recommend reading *The Four Agreements by Don Miguel Ruiz.* There was no intention to copy his work by writing about this concept in this chapter. Ruiz does a much better job at explaining why nothing is personal in a way that is very easy to grasp, and I want to extend credit to Ruiz for highlighting the importance of this topic.

The reason I am including this topic in this book is that this is a very common theme in counseling, and it's a conversation that I have with many clients, especially when they have been impacted by the words and actions of others.

14
ACTIONS SPEAK LOUDER THAN WORDS

What I would like to talk about here is two-fold. The first part is about monitoring your actions. I've already talked about the triangle of thoughts, feelings, and behaviors and how those three things are different yet intertwined. We have our thoughts and beliefs about things; we have our feelings about things, and then we have our behaviors, our responses, and our actions about things.

The second part is about choosing your actions most effectively. Because you're right in a situation doesn't automatically mean that your behavior is effective, and I want to talk about making this distinction so you can choose the most effective response at any given moment.

As I mentioned before, the only thing that will result in any kind of consequence is our actions. You can think about anything you want, and you're allowed to feel whatever it is you're feeling, but it's what you do with those thoughts and feelings that causes consequences.

I can think all day about punching you in the face. Or I can feel angry toward you and feel urges to punch you in the face. However, I'm not going to have any consequences until I punch you in the face.

This is why actions speak louder than words. It is also one of the more consistent things that I see in my practice; when you want to identify patterns of behavior, you don't recognize patterns based on thought or feeling. Patterns emerge, and you recognize these through someone's behaviors.

You can identify this in so many ways. Some classic examples could be an addict who repeatedly says they are going to quit, and this is the last time. However, when the pattern of behavior shows the presence of constant relapse, then there's a greater likelihood that they will relapse again. They may not, but patterns of behavior are more consistent than patterns of intention, which is thought.

Domestic violence is another prime example. Patterns of behavior within the domestic violence cycle are very recognizable. The perpetrator of domestic violence can say that he's going to change, and he is going to work on his behaviors, but until the actions follow, they are empty words and empty promises.

It can be very important to follow patterns of behavior because this is the thing that is most telling about someone and their likelihood for change.

If someone says that they are a nice person but then they treat other people horribly, then their actions indicate that they're not as nice a person as they said they were. It's the behavior that is telling you, and the behaviors say a lot more about that individual. This person could intend to be nice to others, but if their actions contradict their intentions, are they nice?

People don't trust words.
They trust trends in behavior.

A lot of people respond a lot better to actions than words; for example, one of the inmates I worked with was part of my group, and he was learning about coping skills and ways to better manage emotions. One of the topics of the group was communication and interpersonal effectiveness. He'd been estranged from his family and his adult daughter for a while.

This inmate wanted to maintain a relationship with his daughter specifically, and one of the ways he knew how was to tell his family how well he was doing, telling them how much he was learning in groups and trying to convince them that he was on track. However, the problem was that these things didn't carry over so well because they'd heard it all before.

His family members, including his daughter, became fed up to the point that they believed the inmate's words were empty. He'd been trying to convince them for a long time that he was doing better, but he would ultimately give in to behaviors that didn't match his words.

Another indicator to the family that these were empty words was that he wouldn't necessarily ask about them or their day. His interactions were more about trying to convince them how well he was doing. The conversations stayed mostly about him.

During the groups on communication and interpersonal effectiveness, we talked about the importance of validation and listening. We talked about how to rebuild relationships by applying validation. We talked about boundaries and assertive communication, and how to be a better listener.

This inmate started to apply some of these communication skills, and when he was on the phone with his daughter, instead of trying to convince his daughter how great he was doing, the conversation was more about asking about her day. He was asking more about what was going on in her life and using validation by telling her that he was proud of her and giving positive feedback.

During those phone calls, he wouldn't ask for anything in return because this was another common pattern. Quite often, when he called, it was because he needed something, not to ask about how they were doing. Instead, he would ask questions about his family and what was new in their lives. He would leave the conversation with that and hang up without having asked for anything.

The family started to notice this, and they started to see these changes in him. They felt that the changes he was making were now more genuine and that he was doing a lot better because they were seeing his actions, not hearing his words.

It was an interesting dichotomy to witness because the less he tried to convince his family of how well he was doing, the more they were convinced that he was doing better because his actions reflected this. He no longer needed to try to convince them by telling them because his actions became sufficient.

By listening to his family and giving his family his time and attention, the more he was able to rebuild his relationship with them. He reconnected with his daughter, and she became a significant support to him. This was something that he couldn't do in the past.

Actions are what people see. People don't follow your intentions and your thoughts. They don't follow all the things you say you're going to do. People instead notice your patterns of behavior through your actions.

If you want to be a good person, don't tell people how great a person you are. Do good things. If you want to be a likable person, do things that people like. If you want to connect with others, show an interest in them. It's all in the actions.

Your behavior is the only version of you that the world gets to see.

People will get a sense of you based on your actions, not your words. We need to form impressions of the world to make sense of it and to survive, and this goes for people, too. People are unable to form impressions based on your intentions and the thoughts running through your mind. The only thing that people can see about you is your actions.

You can tell everyone you're a hardworking athlete, but until people see the work you've put in and they can see the outcome, this is what they see. It's in the actions.

In the chapter about finding who you are, I talked about how part of finding who you are is more about creating who you are, and this is very relevant here as well. Whatever kind of person you strive to be, it's never about your intentions to be that person. It's not about the desire to be that person. It's not about the fact that one day, you'll be that person. The only way to be the person you desire to be is by doing the things that person would do. It's only in the actions.

One thing that we do have control over is our behavior. I have talked about how we can be more in control of our behaviors when I talked about what happens in the brain in the limbic system and the prefrontal cortex. I talked about how we can become less reactive and be more mindful and intentional in our responses.

Our thoughts are in our control also, but our feelings are not as much because when we feel something in a certain situation, we feel it. It's the way we respond to things. We all have different triggers for our emotions, and it happens. I have also emphasized that whatever anyone ever feels, those feelings are always valid.

Our behaviors, on the other hand, are a choice. We can choose how we're going to respond to a situation, and we choose the actions we take as a result of the things that happen to us. Behaviors are in our control and are also the things that will cause any consequences.

Whatever person you want to create within yourself, you are in control of your actions. You don't become who you want to be by thinking about it. You don't master skills and change behaviors by only imagining them. You have to take action, and this is reflected in your behavior.

The second part of this two-fold chapter about actions is about acting effectively. Whatever your actions are, make sure that your responses are effective. You can do this by beginning to ask yourself what your long-term goal is for the behavior. Are your actions in line with that long-term goal?

Actions are, of course, always more effective than thoughts. Actions are not only the thing that causes consequences, but also the thing that creates results. You have the person who talks about all the great things that they're doing, and then you have the person who is doing all the great things. The person who is taking action doesn't need to talk about it because it's already demonstrated in their actions.

A recurring conversation that comes up in counseling, especially in the context of relationship counseling, is whether it's worth continuing to work on things when a couple has been struggling in their relationship for a while. When couples have been arguing and in conflict for so long, they sometimes get to the point where they don't even know if they want to do the work because they don't know if things will ever get better.

One of the things that I then help clients identify is the trend. What are the trends in behavior? There might still be conflict, but does the trend show the same amount of conflict, less conflict, or more conflict? Quite often, when couples look at their trends, this can be a good indicator of how things are going and how things will look in the future.

For example, in couples counseling, when a couple argues a lot, and there's still a lot of conflict, sometimes when they compare where they are now to where they were, e.g., six months ago, they may notice that even though there is still some present conflict, they are also having conversations about things without fighting. They notice that six months ago they couldn't do this, and so the trend shows that they are increasing their ability to talk to each other and have a conversation with each other without conflict, something they couldn't do six months ago.

They may also notice that the frequency of arguing is less or the intensity of their conflict has gone down. Following that trend, the way that it's currently going would indicate that communication will continue to progress.

On the other hand, there could be a couple or someone who is frustrated in a relationship, and they've been working hard on things, and they identify that they feel as frustrated as ever. They're feeling as upset, and so their trend shows that they still have thoughts of leaving the relationship, and maybe the number of times they're thinking of leaving the relationship has not changed.

This trend indicates that the frustration levels in the relationship are the same and, therefore, no progress is being made. The future trend would, therefore, also indicate that feelings are going to stay approximately the same if the same actions continue.

Now, take a couple where the husband has demonstrated aggressive and angry behaviors, and his wife has gotten to the point where she wants to leave the relationship because of this. Maybe he tells her that he will attend anger management classes and work on his anger, and give him a second chance. This may sound like empty promises, but ultimately, she is going to know if his anger and aggression improve based on his responses, i.e., his actions.

The easiest way to determine this level of progress is to look at the trends of his behavior. Does the husband still flip out over small and insignificant things, or is he better able to manage his responses when he is frustrated? Is he able to apply anger management coping skills when he is angry? When you notice that the trend shows that he is not as reactionary and that he doesn't behave aggressively when upset, this would indicate progress.

You may even notice that there are still outbursts of anger, but you also notice that the frequency of those is now less than it used to be, which indicates progress. Maybe you notice that he can apply mindful breathing skills when he's angry only half of the time. However, maybe a few months ago, he wasn't able to do this at all. His trend would indicate progress.

Over time, you may continue to notice more and more progress, but only the actions will show you this. The trend doesn't consider the intentions and the words, or the promises, only the actions.

If you wonder about whether you're making changes in a certain way and you feel like you want to make progress in a certain area, look at your trends. You can even apply this to the presence of mental health symptoms.

For example, with anxiety, if you experience a lot of anxiety daily and six months later you still experience anxiety, you may not feel like you're making any progress at all. Well, if you explore the trend of your anxiety today compared to six months ago, you may notice that even though you still experience anxiety, you managed to do a lot of things this week that would have been too overwhelming six months before. That indicates a trend of progress, so even though there's still room for more progress, the trend shows that anxiety is getting better.

Actions speak louder than words, and this is a very important thing because we can determine a lot by focusing on actions, whether it's our actions or the actions of others. If you want to understand more about someone else, what do their actions show? If you strive to be a certain way, do your actions reflect this?

15
ACCOUNTABILITY WITHIN CONFLICT

When I talk about relationships and conflict with my clients, one thing I often talk about is validation, which is about being able to hear the other person and working toward an understanding of where they're coming from.

The other part of this is taking accountability, which I talked about when I wrote about identifying the differences between explaining and excusing behavior.

One thing that I see quite a bit in my practice, especially within the context of couples counseling, is that when one person complains about something or brings up an issue, this is usually immediately met with defensiveness. What the defensive individual has not done is listen to the other person and the message they're trying to convey.

Instead, they typically try to justify their behavior. This defensiveness is very consistently one of the biggest responses I've seen, and it seems like people have such difficulty putting their defenses down.

I can spend an entire session in counseling, specifically talking about why not to get defensive, how to listen to the other person, and spend a long time talking about how defensiveness hinders communication and puts up barriers. And even with this conversation, the very next sentence that is spoken is met again with defensiveness. Everything that we talked about goes straight out the window!

I've experienced this several times in sessions, and sometimes, it can be pretty exhausting for everyone involved! This is why I feel the need to talk about this topic.

One of the challenges is to be able to put your defenses down and listen to what the other person is saying, especially if it comes in the form of a complaint. What's important is that instead of being defensive and trying to justify actions, you put your listening cap on. It's important to try to understand the message behind what is being said and not hear the criticism or the judgment.

> Taking accountability doesn't start with explaining your actions. It starts with listening to how your actions made someone else feel.

For example, say your spouse is complaining that you're such a slob! They're complaining that the kitchen is always a mess, and they're so tired of having to clean up after you. They're pointing out how you always leave the dishes in the sink and never put things away. Well, of course, it would be very easy to become defensive in a situation like this because you're being accused, and they're pointing fingers at you.

Now your defenses are high because you're being called a slob, they think you're lazy, and fingers are being pointed at you. But what you haven't done is listen to the message of your spouse about walking into a dirty kitchen every day, recognizing that something you're doing is genuinely bothering them.

And this is the key. When it comes to conflict, the key thing is being able to listen and understand what is going on instead of becoming defensive about the complaint.

For example, if someone is grouchy and you ask them a question, maybe they give you a snappy response and act irritated toward you. Your response in your mind may be something along the lines of well, fine if you're going to talk to me like that, then screw you too. Now you're defensive and irritated back at the person, and now there's room for conflict because you're now both defensive and irritable.

You're now both very reactive, and you give the same level of defensiveness back, and now you're both arguing. But what you didn't do was look past their behavior and look at the message.

If you asked that person a question and their response in their irritated state was something like: "Oh my God, I don't know, okay? Whatever!" then a healthier, more compassionate, and understanding way of responding could be an acknowledgment of their shortness and to ask if everything is okay. Maybe you could even offer support.

You can't solve a problem you're not listening to.

So instead of not becoming defensive and not taking their curt response to you personally, you're able to put your defenses aside, and you can look past their response and identify that maybe they're responding to something that has nothing to do with you.

So, instead of getting upset in return, now you can change your approach and be more compassionate. This can only happen when you're not defensive because you're not taking the response personally. This is the thing that is consistently lacking when it comes to arguments and people voicing their complaints to one another.

It's very natural to react defensively when someone is pointing out something about you that they don't like. It's our instinct kicking in because we want to save our egos. We have an ingrained need to protect our ego, and therefore, in response, we come up with an excuse or a justification for why we did certain things. Instead, one of the challenges I have for you is to put that defensiveness aside and to listen to the complaint or what the other person is saying.

When you hear the complaint, and you allow yourself to hear what the other is saying, you may even be able to take accountability and ask yourself if you do have some part to play in the other person's complaint.

I remember when my twin sister and I were arguing, and we were maybe nine to ten years old. When things were heated, and we were not nice to each other (which was very rare, fortunately), I would say very mean things to her. I wasn't even thinking about what I was saying, I knew we were angry with each other for some reason or other.

One day, she asked me why I always said mean and hurtful things to her. She pointed out that even when we were arguing and angry with each other, she still wouldn't say things to hurt me, but I would always say things to hurt her.

In this situation, I could have easily become defensive and retorted by saying that wasn't true, but it caught me so off guard that I realized that she was right, and the things that I said were, in fact, very hurtful. I was able to take that accountability and hear what it was she was saying rather than becoming defensive.

One of the things that we're consistently not good at is staying rational and objective when things are painful and hurtful or when faced with criticism and judgment. These things cloud our ability to see the bigger picture and look objectively at what is being said. It clouds our ability to hear the message that is in the words.

But when you can do this, it becomes a beautiful thing. It's too easy to respond negatively when someone is upset with you and to be negative and reactive back. But wouldn't it be more effective to see past that and recognize that when someone is hurt or when they're complaining or bringing up a concern, this is a valid thing?

When engaged in couples counseling, one person says that every time they try to bring up a certain subject, it's because that subject is important to them. They want to be able to talk about it, but the other person shuts them down all the time.

A typical response in a situation like this is a justification for shutting the person down because there's no point in talking about this thing. But again, what they haven't done is listen to what the other person has said. What they haven't heard is that this particular subject is an important thing for their partner.

Instead of hearing that message and responding in a way that acknowledges that this topic is important for their partner and working toward having a conversation about it because it's important, the response is one of defensiveness.

They may tell their partner that they don't think it's important because they won't get anywhere. This happens because every time they have a conversation, it leads to arguments. So, what's the point in even talking about this? Now, the initial feelings are being dismissed and shut down, creating a conflict.

Here's a rule of thumb. If something is important to one person, and that person is important to you, then the things they find important become important to you too.

Another thing that happens a lot in couples counseling is, for example, when one person suggests something to the other. Maybe they're telling their partner that they should try this thing, or they give some kind of advice or suggestion that the other person should try out. Typically, the advice is shot down and dismissed. This is because of the underlying power struggle that is present in conflict. However, when anybody else in the world (for example, the counselor, some random person on TV, or a friend) gives them the same advice or suggestion, all of a sudden, it sounds like a great idea. And now the partner who made the same suggestion in the first place is left incredibly frustrated and angry because it's the same thing they suggested, but it was dismissed.

When a partner gives advice that is immediately dismissed, but the same advice is accepted by anybody else, it signals a power struggle. The underlying dynamic is this: if I follow your suggestion, it means you were right, and I was wrong. That would make me lose face, and I can't let you win the power struggle, so I reject your advice.

This sounds incredibly childish, I know, but this is exactly the power struggle dynamic that is present with many couples.

We've probably all experienced a situation like this where we reject something simply because it came from a specific person. But had this come from anybody else, then we would have accepted it.

We turn things down a lot, or we don't want to hear the message, but I think it's important that we do. I also believe it would help alleviate a lot of conflict because when we can hear a complaint, then we can problem-solve those, and we can work toward a resolution.

However, if we're dismissing people's complaints, then there's no room for any resolution, and the issues are going to continue, and then the conflict continues.

When couples have recurring conflicts, one typical response from one-half of the couple is something along the lines of: "Oh my God, I wish you would stop going on and on about this one thing!" Well, why do you think they are going on and on about the same thing? It's because this thing is unresolved! There wouldn't be a need for this person to ask something over and over if they received a response!

When someone asks you a question, and later, they ask you again, and then again, this can be incredibly frustrating. Your defensive response would be very quick to tell that person to stop bugging you! However, the likely reason they're asking you this question over and over is that instead of answering the question, you complained about it instead!

This turns into a no-win situation because the person who is asking isn't getting an answer, so they're frustrated, and they're advocating for themselves by asking again. But you're also frustrated because they're asking the same question over and over. The missing piece to this perpetual cycle is being able to put defenses down and listen to the question.

The same happens frequently in conflict. Your initial response to someone complaining is to think, "Here they go again. Blah, blah, blah! Complaining all the time..." However, if you sat and listened to the complaints instead of complaining about the complaints, if you listened to what this complaining was about, then you can work together to resolve these, and guess what? The complaining would stop!

When couples get so frustrated with each other because they hear whining and complaining, they shut down. When they shut down, then still nothing gets resolved, and so the conflict continues and comes up again and again. This is the recurring cycle, and it's important to get out of this cycle.

If you want to work toward resolving conflict, whether it's in your relationship or a different type of relationship, one of the clues to look for is to recognize the recurring and common complaints that often come up. Whenever you find yourself thinking along the lines of "Ugh! Here they go again, they're talking about this again," this is a clue that, first of all, you're not listening, and secondly, the complaint of the other is not resolved.

A much more productive approach in a situation like this is to acknowledge the complaint, then address the complaint, and now you can work on problem-solving.

When you sit down and address the complaint instead of complaining about someone complaining, you can identify what the complaint or concern is. You can identify the issue. Once the issue has been identified, you can work together to resolve this.

This can only happen when defenses are down and accountability is up. Without this, you cannot work on resolving issues because you're too busy justifying your responses. When you can resolve the recurring issues, they don't have to come up again.

The other factor about the importance of putting your defenses down, taking accountability, and addressing concerns is that the person doing the complaining is going to feel heard and validated, and this is going to help build a connection.

I can tell you that when you have complaints and concerns, and you bring them up to the person who can help resolve them, and they're being dismissed repeatedly, then that leads to resentment. Those resentments, in turn, create conflict, and this is when you get into power struggles, and those are all the dynamics that increase conflict.

Like I said before, it's incredibly difficult to put your defensiveness aside because doing so involves the need to swallow your pride. But this needs to happen for the sake of the relationship. It's important to be able to take a step back and acknowledge that you're not losing a power struggle. You're not losing face by acknowledging that someone else's complaint is valid. Instead, you're working toward resolving issues and working through concerns, and this is a much more rewarding and empowering place to be.

If you're able to put some of your defenses aside, you can swallow your pride and listen to the other person. I can guarantee that you're going to get much better results. You're being a lot more effective.

Of course, this goes both ways. If you're the one with the concern or a complaint, or you need to bring up an issue that is bothering you, and you want to talk about it, but you're getting dismissed over and over, then, of course, you're going to become resentful as well. You're likely going to become frustrated with the person who isn't listening, and you build resentment about the situation.

Of course, you're going to be frustrated and exhausted because your issue remains unresolved. But when your partner listens to your complaint, hears it, and acknowledges it and wants to work on resolving this with you, then you can voice the things that bother you, which makes you feel heard and validated.

Communication will improve because you feel heard and validated. You feel supported, and feelings like these are going to increase your security within the relationship. When you feel heard and validated in your complaints, then you know you can come to the person to address issues, and this will build connection and security with both partners in the relationship.

One of the clues to pay attention to is the recurring complaints, and when the tendency is to reject the complaints because you've heard it all before, instead of having this defensive and dismissive approach, I challenge you to listen to what is being said.

Another thing that can happen, another form of defensiveness, is deflection. When someone complains about something that you do, there's a good likelihood that you will, in turn, point out something that the other person is doing wrong.

This is a deflection and is not productive in any way. If this tends to happen, I would suggest staying focused on the initial concerns, and if other issues are brought up, they can be addressed after the initial concerns are resolved.

Deflection is not problem-solving,
it's problem-swapping.

For example, if you bring up a concern that the kitchen is always a mess and it makes cooking dinner harder because you have to clean the entire kitchen first, and the response is that the fact that you never pick your laundry up off the floor is highlighted, then you can respond by suggesting to address and resolve the kitchen problem first, and then you can both address the laundry problem.

In this way, you're still staying focused on the subject. Deflection is such a common defense tactic and often does not result in any resolution because instead of problem-solving, now everyone is only focused on the other's wrongdoings, and the issues are being avoided.

Being able to identify when defenses are high and put these aside and work on listening instead of justifying is such a valuable thing, and I believe that a lot of conflict would be resolved by the presence of this shift in response. It's probably the single biggest barrier that I experience when conflict and the inability to resolve issues are present, and therefore, the need to highlight this recurring and important topic is very necessary.

16
DECISION MAKING

This chapter addresses indecisiveness, something, of course, that many people experience, not only in a counseling setting. Sometimes, we can be in a situation where no decision feels right. It could be that we feel stuck in a situation, and we're confused about what to do.

In a situation like this, there are several options and ways to explore the best ways to make decisions, and I would like to highlight some of these options in this chapter. I also know that decision-making is a very personal and subjective experience, and what I don't want to do here is tell you how to make your decisions! I recognize that there are very many personality styles, and different approaches work for different people. I want to present some approaches that may help you in your process.

If you're in a situation and you don't know what to do and it feels like there's no good outcome, one approach is to not make any big decisions at all. If you're stuck between different choices and none of those decisions interest you or feel good, then maybe none of those at that time is the right decision.

This may seem intuitive or simple, but it's surprising how many people will decide because they're fed up with a situation, or they make an impulsive decision because they are being reactive.

Of course, the option of not making any big decisions at the moment is only appropriate if there is no real timeline attached to your situation. Some examples of these types of situations are choosing to move to a new area, feeling dissatisfied with your relationship, or wondering about leaving your job.

Another option open to you to help you decide is to follow your bliss. Be guided by what excites you and follow what you feel is important to you.

The decision is, of course, simple when out of the two options in front of you (staying or leaving), one feels very right, and the other feels very wrong. Of course, you'd be encouraged to go with the decision that feels right for you, but this is not what I'm talking about. It's precisely that lack of clarity that makes you unable to move forward with a choice.

Decision-making is a personal and subjective experience.
What works for one may not work for another.

When it comes to following your bliss - things you want to do and things that excite you - this can happen in two different ways. This can be done by identifying the things that create excitement in the long-term or that excite you now.

When you identify things in the long-term, you focus on your goals and your dreams, and you work on pursuing those. You can then make a new plan of action based on where it will lead you in the future. This could be a business plan or a personal goal but identifying what your future goals are and then deciding based on which path best gets you there is one approach.

One personal example of this is when I worked in community

mental health as a counselor; I already identified that my long-term career goal was to become self-employed. The Assistant Behavioral Health Director position at the community mental health center opened, and I applied for it. In the meantime, I presented at a local conference and was approached by someone who offered me a contract to run groups at the correctional institution in town.

I was eventually offered the Assistant Behavioral Health Director position, but was also offered the corrections contract, and there was no way I could do both. I loved the idea of doing either of those, and I felt pretty stuck on which decision to make.

I then focused on my long-term career goals and identified that this included being self-employed. The Assistant Behavioral Health Director position would keep me employed full-time in the long-term. However, the offer from corrections was contract-based, and therefore, it would allow me to open a private practice while still having a steady income from the contract.

This was the deciding factor for me, and I chose to work the contract in corrections. It eventually allowed me to transition to private practice and expand my self-employment. When my contract ended in 2019, I transitioned to a full-time self-employed private practice, and I am now in the position I wished to be all those years ago. It was focusing on my long-term goals that helped me make the right decision.

The other option is to focus on the things that excite you in your current situation. When you identify the things that excite you in your current situation, you can also explore where those interests come from. Maybe you're excited about moving in a whole different direction, like wanting to focus on study rather than work, or wanting to pursue a whole new career path. When we use our emotions to identify our passions and joys, but also our reasons for how to get there, we often have a more balanced and stable foundation, which can lead to healthier outcomes.

Another way to approach your situation is to identify the positives that are still present in your situation. This could be identifying the one to two colleagues that you can still laugh and joke with at work, or maybe it's the income and financial stability. Shifting your focus is also about recognizing the things in your situation that you're grateful for or that are still going well.

Sometimes, when we're in a stressful situation, it can be difficult to distinguish the positives from the negatives. Quite often, we engage in all-or-nothing thinking and think that our entire situation is bad and that everything about our situation sucks. This leads to feeling overwhelmed, which in turn leads to paralysis in decision-making.

When we can explore our situation and begin to identify what aspects we're specifically struggling with, we can focus on only those. So, there are several different ways to make decisions when you're unsure about what to do, especially when nothing feels right. When you're able to identify that there are still positive aspects of your situation, e.g., you get along well with certain colleagues, or you value your financial stability, then you may be able to specifically address the aspects of the situation that need improvement and focus on those.

The right decision is often the one that aligns with your future self, not your current frustration.

Applying gratitude can also cause a shift in our perspective on our situation. The concept of gratitude can sometimes sound dismissive or insincere, but one thing that happens when gratitude is present is that it begins to open doors for something better. In my experience, our mindsets play a huge role in the opportunities we create for ourselves, and I have seen time and time again that when someone begins to acknowledge the positive aspects of a situation or begins to apply gratitude to their situation, new doors open for them.

I'm not sure how much you believe in the Law of Attraction, but there's one quote by Abraham Hicks that says: "You can't get to where you want to go by trying to get away from where you are because trying to leave one place puts you in resistance and won't let you go to another place. You have to love the best things about where you are, which opens the doors to even better."

It's this same idea that if you're stuck in a situation, but work on recognizing the positives within your situation, and then you move because of better opportunities, then you set yourself up for greater success.

Take, for example, people who run away from themselves. Running away from yourself doesn't work at all. Someone might be sick of everything; they don't like anything, their job sucks, their friends suck, their whole situation sucks, the area they live in sucks. Maybe because of this, they decide to start over. What often happens, though, is that they find that it doesn't make them any happier when they do move away and start over. This is not because everything didn't suck; maybe it did. However, part of the reason why everything was bad was because of their outlook.

Maybe things sucked because their perspective was negative, and they didn't allow themselves to see the positive aspects of their situation. We see the world through the lens that we carry, and if our lens includes a lot of judgment, criticism of others, and negativity, then we're most likely going to home in on those negative aspects of any situation.

If that negative lens is a part of them, then it doesn't matter where they decide to have their fresh start. The same situation is going to come up again.

When you make decisions, those decisions shouldn't come from negative mindsets. Decisions are usually better when positive mindsets are present. When you leave a job, is it because you're working toward a better job, or is it because you're overwhelmed at the moment and simply decide to quit?

When it comes to making significant decisions, it's about recognizing what isn't working. Boundaries are also important. If you're in a situation where your boundaries are being violated repeatedly and your boundaries are not being honored and validated, this would be a good indicator to leave the situation behind.

When you identify the aspects of your situation that are not working for you, then you're left with the things that are okay or positive. And when you identify the aspects that are not healthy for you, then you begin to apply healthier boundaries around those.

Weighing out the pros and cons can be another very helpful skill. It's important to identify not only the pros of each choice but also the disadvantages, and when you create a visual of the effects of each choice, one may stand out more. You may be able to identify significantly more pros or cons on each side, which could help in decision-making.

Even identifying a timeline can be helpful. I talked about the importance and benefits of identifying a timeline in a previous chapter, but this can also be helpful in a situation where decisions are hard. For example, if you're not happy at your job but think you may be able to address some of the more difficult aspects of your job and thereby improve your job satisfaction, then setting a timeline to highlight this can be helpful.

When you give yourself a timeline for, e.g., three months from now and three months later, you recognize that you're as miserable in your job, then maybe you also identify that this trend is not going to change, and it's time to leave for something better.

Hopefully, I have presented several different tools to help with decision-making. I can present these tools to you to facilitate your decision-making, but ultimately, you are the only person who can make those decisions for yourself.

17
FORGIVENESS

Forgiveness is a topic that is prevalent in counseling sessions because it's often very hard to let go of the past. The inability to let go is often accompanied by shoulda/woulda/coulda's or what-ifs. It's also accompanied by regrets. It comes with hurt, with pain. There are so many difficult emotions that go along with the inability to let go.

Forgiveness becomes an important topic in the session, but I also feel like forgiveness is a very misunderstood concept. In my experience, when a lot of people think about forgiveness, or when they hear about forgiveness, they think that this means that whatever happened is okay. But this is not what forgiveness is.

In my experience, a lot of people think forgiveness is about forgetting, like pretending that whatever happened never did, or that it involves having to have a clean slate, which is also absolutely not what forgiveness is.

In my experience, when people feel like they need to forgive, they feel like they need to "give in," or if something has a power struggle dynamic, forgiving is about giving in to whatever took place. They mistakenly believe that forgiving means they're allowing people to walk all over them, but this is also not what forgiveness is.

These are a few of the common misconceptions that make it incredibly difficult for people to apply forgiveness. Of course you wouldn't want to forgive someone if it meant you had to forget what they did; this would be very dismissive. Of course you wouldn't be able to forgive if it meant you had to be okay with what happened.

There may be many books on the topic of forgiveness, but I want to talk about forgiveness in the way it manifests in my practice. This may not be the true definition of forgiveness, or forgiveness experts may even disagree. If you want to know more about forgiveness and you feel like this is one area that you need specific help with, I recommend further reading that focuses specifically on forgiveness.

The way forgiveness manifests in my practice is both forgiveness toward others as well as forgiveness toward the self.

> You can forgive someone
> and still place healthy boundaries.

I'll begin by highlighting a story of forgiveness that happened in one of my group sessions. I used to run a weekly grief counseling group in an inpatient residential substance abuse treatment center, and I would be willing to argue that anyone who is undergoing treatment at an inpatient facility is experiencing some type of grief and loss.

One quick thing about grief, in particular, is that grief is not about the loss of people. People can mourn the loss of things, jobs, the loss of the substance they are working on recovering from, abandonment by family and friends, etc. There are so many ways that grief manifests in our lives.

In the grief group, I was allowing people to participate whose grief and loss were not limited to death. I remember one woman who was in the group, and she talked about grieving the loss of her children because, through her addiction, her children were taken from her by child protective services.

Her children were now in foster care, so she was angry at the world and the system. In the group, she shared her story about not having much of a role-model because her mom had struggled in many ways, and she had been in and out of the system.

She talked about her mom's struggle with addiction and how she had been neglected and was partly raised in the foster system. She talked about the anger she held toward her mom for doing so, knowing it was a major reason why she had struggled to be a good mom and why her children were now in foster care.

As she shared her anger with the group, she asked the common questions, "Shouldn't a mom provide for her children? Shouldn't she have been the most important thing to her mom? How could these random men and her lifestyle be more appealing than her child?"

As she was able to talk about her grief, she received a lot of validation and support from her peers. Then we talked about her children and how she wanted them to understand that she's in recovery and that she's doing the best that she can. She wanted her children to understand that she didn't get the best role-modeling from her mom, and this led to her numbing her emotions through addiction.

I started to identify an interesting parallel where her and her mom's lives were very similar. Their lives reflected each other in many ways, e.g., they both had children, both of their children were in child protective services and in and out of the foster system, they both struggled with addiction, and both had a history of unhealthy relationships and questionable people in the home.

However, she had a lot of anger toward her mom for her mom going through all of this, yet she wanted her children to forgive her for what she had done. She wanted her children to understand where she was coming from and why she did the things she did.

During the group, I validated her and pointed out that under the circumstances, she was doing the best that she could. She had turned to drugs because her emotions and experiences became too overwhelming, and she didn't know how else to deal with them. She felt a lot of pain, hurt, and anger, which she was numbing, which was the best coping skill she had at the time.

She'd never learned any coping skills on how to deal with emotional volatility. She'd never experienced any real role-modeling on how to raise children, so she did the best she knew how, based on the role-modeling she received from her mom.

She could see for herself that she had done the best she could with her children. She did the best she could with the knowledge she had at the time and given her situation at the time. And this is the understanding, the forgiveness she needed from her children because she hadn't known better.

Then I suggested to her that maybe her mom needed the same thing from her. Maybe her mom also did the absolute best she knew how with what she knew and with what she had. Maybe her mom also never had role-modeling from her parents, and she wanted that same level of understanding from her.

This was when the lightbulb went on for her. Suddenly, she realized that what she was asking of her children, her mom was asking of her. She realized at that moment that she expected her children, still as children, to give her something that she, as an adult, couldn't give.

When we judge past choices, we're doing so with information we didn't have then.

When she made this realization, the change in her was instant. She could now understand at that moment that her mom was as broken as she was, and this is when her healing journey started.

Her anger began to dissipate because she could understand that her mom was in the same position that she was at the time. In that moment of realization, everything changed for her.

This, to me, is what forgiveness looks like.

I wrote earlier in this book about needing to make a distinction between excusing a behavior vs. explaining a behavior. When this client started the practice of forgiving her mom, she also acknowledged that this was not an excuse for her mom's behavior.

She could discern that her mom's struggles were not an excuse to be brought up in a broken home. It was not an excuse to be exposed to an environment with drug prevalence or questionable partners. It was an explanation for why her mom made the choices she did, but it wasn't an excuse.

At the same time, this client wasn't forgetting what happened either. She could acknowledge that she could still place healthy boundaries with her mom because even though she could now understand her mom's behaviors, it didn't mean they were starting over like nothing had happened.

I want to talk about a very important aspect of forgiveness. One of the things we have to realize when we're working on forgiving someone, or ourselves, is that we're always doing the best we can *with the knowledge that we have at the time, the mindset we're in at the time, and with the situation that we're in at the time.*

Many times, when we hold regrets, or when we tell ourselves that we should've done something, or somebody else should've done something, we're only ever applying that with the current knowledge we now have.

If I tell myself that I should've left half an hour earlier today, then I would have spared myself the extra stress on the road this morning. Well, I'm only saying this because I learned after the fact that all this extra traffic stress was going to happen, but I didn't know it at the time.

Or maybe I tell myself that I should've taken this other class instead of the one I'm taking now because the teacher of the other class turned out to be so much better, well I'm only applying this "shoulda" to my life once I learned how the teacher was as the class progressed. I didn't have this knowledge when I chose my classes.

When you have regrets, you're holding the fact that you're not psychic against yourself! It's like buying a lottery ticket, and when the lottery numbers come out, you tell yourself that you should've put those six numbers on when you purchased the lottery ticket! If you had put those numbers on, then you would've won all that money!

The thing is, you can only have regrets with current knowledge. It's very unfair to judge yourself and regret things and hold things against yourself, with the knowledge that you didn't have at the time.

When it comes to forgiveness, I believe that this is a core element. I believe that regardless of whatever decision was made, it was made at that time with only the knowledge that was present at that time.

In my experience, this is the piece that many people don't take into consideration—for example, an inmate who has hurt someone. As weird as it sounds, they were even doing the best that they could with the knowledge and circumstances that they had at the time.

If someone is ready to hurt someone else, they feel like that's the best thing they know to do in that moment—for example, someone who robs a bank. We know that robbing a bank is wrong! How would anyone ever think that's the best decision? Well, somewhere in their mind, they did feel like that was the best choice they had, with all the knowledge they had at that time, because otherwise, they would not have made that decision if they felt that there was a better alternative.

One story that one of the inmates relayed to me about his past was that when he was sixteen, he had an older girlfriend, and he told me that he was a victim of statutory rape. His girlfriend became pregnant, but instead of the statutory rape being highlighted, he was ordered to pay child support by the court. He was forced by probation to get a job because of the child support.

In his sixteen-year-old brain, after experiencing an injustice by the system and not being heard by the system at all, he came to the outlook of fuck the system. The system completely failed him, and from then, he decided to do everything to screw the system over because that was what he knew was the best thing for him at the time, in his state of mind, knowledge, and emotions he had at that time.

The knowledge he had at that time was that the whole system screwed him over, and so he was going to screw them over. So even though many of the following decisions that he made were criminal, because by our standards they are wrong and by our judgments and perspective they are wrong, his knowledge and outlook were not the same.

A consideration that is important when people make all sorts of decisions is that they are always doing this from their perspective. When we judge something or someone, we're always judging them based on our current knowledge and our current perspective. So, of course, we can see that some decisions are not the right decisions because we can see the circumstances through our lens.

However, we're not considering the decision maker's circumstances and their point of view, their limitations and beliefs, their emotional state, and all the factors that contribute to their state of mind in that moment in time.

For example, take someone who chooses to do drugs. Well, you and I would, of course, never choose to do drugs. We would have the clarity to say, "Why would I want to put a needle with heroin in my arm? Why would I choose to engage in something that I know is going to ruin my life? Why would I ever choose that?" Well, that's a great point. We wouldn't because we're making this determination with our current knowledge, and we know what's best for us.

However, if we're broken, if we believe that we're not worthy of love or anything good, and if this belief has been reinforced time and time again throughout our life, and we've been abused in many different ways and emotional pain is chronic, well maybe then, that needle of numbing heroin sounds quite comforting in that state of mind.

When we judge another person for choosing to use drugs, we're not considering any of their circumstances. We're only judging them since we wouldn't do it, so why would they? Well, because their perspective is very different.

In my experience, forgiveness consists of a few different things. One of those things is that you need to consider that a choice is coming from the other person's perspective. Whatever you're not able to forgive someone for, it's because you're looking at the situation through your lens. You're looking at the situation from your perspective and knowledge and placing this on someone else.

To be able to forgive someone includes putting yourself in their shoes and working toward understanding where they're coming from. That does not mean that you have to agree with it. It also does not excuse a behavior. But when you put yourself in someone else's shoes and consider their thoughts, their feelings, their set of circumstances, and everything that led up to their decision at that moment, then if you can work toward an understanding, an explanation of their choices and why that person made those choices, you also have to take yourself out of your perspective first.

Another factor of forgiveness is about recognizing that when someone is deciding, it's the best decision they are making for themselves at that time. If someone is yelling at their kids, it's because they are possibly overwhelmed, their patience capacity is gone, and maybe they've tried being nice, but at that moment, being overwhelmed now, the only way they know how to direct their kids' behavior is to yell. Again, it does not excuse the behavior, but it does allow you to understand why they are doing this.

The same goes for the bully in the playground who shows aggressive behaviors. Is that the best decision they are making for themselves at that moment in time? Yes, for them, because in that moment, they may feel the need to be aggressive, or they've learned to be aggressive because, in that moment, those aggressive behaviors are keeping them safe.

You and I wouldn't choose to be aggressive, and we may think this is a horrible thing to do, and we would never choose to voluntarily treat other people this way. We're also able to say this because we haven't been hurt by getting close to others, and we don't need to place this protection layer on ourselves. We haven't had the same life experiences as the bully.

Forgiveness is about being able to consider that if we were in that person's shoes and had the same upbringing and the same horrible experiences as all the people around us, then maybe we would also be aggressive. You're taking yourself out of your shoes and putting yourself in the other person's shoes, and now you understand why someone is making their choices.

At that moment in time, you may come to understand that the aggressive bully doesn't know how to speak nicely, or they've never learned how to assert their needs appropriately because they've never had an opportunity to practice this, or when they have tried to practice assertive communication then others have abused that privilege, so they've come to learn that assertive communication doesn't work.

Maybe over time, the bully learns about assertive communication and then looks back and tells themselves that they should never have treated others this way. But they can only say this because they are seeing this now from their current perspective, and that's when they can see the situation differently.

This is one thing that comes up in my counseling sessions a lot. Many people have regrets, and they tell themselves that they should've done something differently. Then I point out to them that the simple fact that they can acknowledge that they should've done something differently indicates growth!

The fact that you can see that something should've been different indicates that you are in a different mind state than you used to be, and this indicates that there has been a change in outlook.

Even though you may have regrets over the past, the fact that you see it differently and that you wouldn't make the same choice today, and for the simple fact that you're telling yourself you should've done something else instead, means there's growth.

This reframe can be very helpful. If I'm horrible to people all the time, I don't care about people because nobody in my life has been nice to me, then to me, that's what works. It's the best way I know how to be, and it's how I know to protect myself from others. But then, over time, I learned that this is no longer effective, and I learned how to be better at communication. I began to learn how to build meaningful relationships and how to seek out healthy people in my life. I learned how to place healthier boundaries and communicate with people who are good for me.

Well, maybe then I look back and think, oh wow, I was a horrible person! I should never have been that mean to people! Well, first of all, that judgment of "shouldn't have been mean" is with the new knowledge. You're adding your current knowledge onto a past expectation of yourself, and that's not fair because you didn't have that knowledge at that time. So, to hold that against yourself is saying you should've been psychic, and you're telling yourself that you should've known the knowledge that was to come in the future! This is completely unreasonable!

Second, even saying to yourself that you should've been a certain way in the past indicates that you're looking at the past from a newfound perspective, and that right there shows growth, change, and learning.

So, how do you even begin to forgive someone who hurt you? It begins with you working toward an understanding of where that individual was coming from. You begin to understand why they made that decision. It doesn't mean that you come to agree with what they did. It doesn't mean that you come to like what they did. It doesn't mean that you come to think their choice was okay. It also doesn't mean that you forget about it.

Say, for example, I have a babysitter who has been babysitting for me regularly. Then, over time, I notice that, now and then, some cash is going missing, and then maybe some other things go missing. I finally catch on that it's my babysitter who is stealing from me.

Then, I confront my babysitter and ask them about the missing cash and items. Maybe the babysitter confesses and says they're sorry, they did take the money, but only because they didn't have enough money to cover their bills or to feed their kids. Maybe they tell me they had a major car repair they couldn't afford, and it was an unexpected expense, so if they took a little bit of cash here and there from me, I wouldn't notice, and they intended to replace the cash.

I can understand where my babysitter is coming from. I can see the reasoning behind why they stole from me. I can hear their explanation, and I can be empathetic to their motif for doing this. I can forgive them for taking my money because I understand why.

However, does that excuse the behavior? Absolutely not. Does that mean that I have to forget about what happened? Also no. Does it mean that we can start over as a clean slate and pretend nothing ever happened? Definitely not. I can forgive my babysitter and at the same time tell them they are no longer welcome in my house. I can forgive them and still place new boundaries with them because even though they are forgiven, the circumstances are now different.

This is one common misconception that a lot of people who have been forgiven make. They often believe that because someone has forgiven their behaviors, they can start again, or things are back to the way before, but this is not what forgiveness means. If you find yourself angry that someone says they have forgiven you but still don't want you around, then it doesn't mean they haven't forgiven you. It means that they have forgiven you *and* adjusted their boundaries with you accordingly because they have still learned from the situation.

So, because you forgive, it doesn't mean that you must let hurtful people back into your life. Forgiveness is not the same as forgetting. Forgiveness does not mean starting over. You forgive, but you still learn.

18

ASSERTIVENESS AND CONFIDENCE

In this chapter, I would like to talk about assertive communication and make distinctions between assertive communication, passive communication, and aggressive communication.

Assertive communication is the preferred communication style because you stand up for your needs, but you also consider the needs of others. This includes speaking up for yourself and establishing and standing up for your boundaries.

People who have difficulty establishing boundaries tend to have a more passive communication style. They tend to have a harder time saying no, or they find it more difficult to stand up for their needs, especially if they believe that this may lead to conflict. They may then not assert themselves because they associate standing up for themselves with a possible argument that they want to avoid.

This difficulty with asserting needs could be with strangers, but also with people you know.

Assertive communication is not only about standing up for your needs and boundaries, but also about doing this effectively. When you stand up for yourself in an aggressive way, this communication is forceful. People who tend to have more passive communication may believe that assertive communication is aggressive communication, but they are very different.

Assertive communicators can communicate their needs without being abrupt about it. For example, say you're standing in line at the checkout at the grocery store, and someone cuts in front of you. A passive communicator may not say anything, and they may be irritated about it. An aggressive communicator may be too forceful and may immediately become argumentative about it, but an assertive communicator may say something like, "Excuse me, I believe the line is right behind me," or "Excuse me, I believe I was next in line after that person."

**Assertive isn't aggressive;
it's direct and respectful.**

If you tend to be more of a passive individual and communicating assertively even in a situation like this may feel overwhelming, then one tactic you may be able to use that might make it a little easier is to ask a question about the situation. In this way, you take the approach like you're not sure. Taking the example of somebody cutting in line, you could say, "Excuse me, is this the line, or did the line start back there?"

When you assert yourself but with an air of confusion, this approach may be easier for more passive communicators. When you assert your needs through a question rather than a statement, it leaves less room for defensiveness from the other individual, and this reduces the risk of conflict.

There are so many variations of doing things. For example, you do something that your boss has asked you to do, and you know that you did it right, but then your boss tries to tell you that you did it wrong. A passive communicator may not say anything or may not stand up for themselves. However, when you address this with the approach of trying to clarify the situation with a question, you may get a better response. For instance, "Wait a minute, when you asked me to work on this project, this is what you needed from me, right?" Then, if your boss confirms that, you can tell them this is what you did and assert yourself.

Another thing that goes a long way with assertive communication is confidence. Confidence may have to start in a "fake it till you make it" sense, but one thing that I have repeatedly observed is that people respond to confidence.

For example, if your boss tells you that you need to present something for your team in next week's staff meeting, you may become very anxious about this. You may then go to the next staff meeting and have no idea what you're saying. This may then reflect in your body language and non-verbal communication, saying things like, "I know I need to speak about this, but I'm a little nervous, so bear with me!" or "This is a little intimidating for me!"

> Body language and tone matter just as much as your actual words when enforcing a boundary.

When you start communicating in this way and with these types of phrases, you may feel like you're getting sympathy from the audience, but most of the time, you're not. What you're getting is a loss of confidence in your ability to speak about your subject well.

If you find yourself in the same situation and you have no idea what you're talking about or you're very nervous, I challenge you to go in there with body language that reflects confidence and communicate what you need to say with confidence in your tone of voice and eye contact.

I also challenge you to not make excuses for things, like "Yeah, I'm not prepared. I couldn't find much about the subject." With an air of confidence, you may instead say, "Well, I did some research, and what I came up with about the subject was the best that I could find."

People respond to body language and non-verbal communication. When you talk confidently, people respond because they know you mean business. If you talk in a way like you've already drawn your conclusions, this will be perceived as confidence by others because they perceive that you know what you're talking about.

Taking the example of being cut off in line at the grocery store, when you use this same level of confident non-verbal communication where you are confident in your conclusions, e.g., "Excuse me, I believe the line is over there," then that comes across as more serious. It shows the other person that you know what you're talking about and it's a lot more effective in getting the desired response than nervous and insecure communication.

This confidence in body language and non-verbal communication is effective, especially when advocating for your needs. It makes your message come across a lot more clearly.

Confidence is reflected in your body language, your tone of voice, the level of eye contact, and your body posture. For example, if you need a day off work, and you ask your boss in a very nervous way, you avoid eye contact and speak in a meek voice, your request may not be taken as seriously. However, if you ask your boss with firm eye contact and you communicate with confident body language that you have something very important to you, and can you please have this day off, then this request is going to be taken more seriously.

This also applies when saying no. When you say no to someone but at the same time, you're hesitant about it, or you show some reservation or insecurity about saying no, then your "no" may not be taken as seriously. This may result in people pushing your boundaries.

However, if you tell the person with confidence no, you're not able to do this, and you say this more assertively, with confidence, then this request is more likely to be met, but also respected more because of the way you conveyed your "no."

Body language that goes along with someone who knows what they are saying or who is confident is reflected in straight shoulders, a straighter body posture, and firm eye contact.

When you have more passive communication, then body language tends to come with a lowered head and shoulders hunched over more. You may be more fidgety, and your voice is not as strong. There may be more hesitation, more time taken before speaking, making excuses for things, or apologizing.

When you want your body language and non-verbal communication to align with confidence, begin with your posture. Hold your back straight and your shoulders straight, and address the person you're talking to. Look at them and make eye contact because it tells them that you're addressing them with confidence.

The same applies to your tone of voice. When you use a stronger voice with fewer hesitations and less "err, umm," your voice carries better, and your confidence comes across more.

One of the interesting things about assertive communication is that it can have a snowball effect. I've witnessed this a lot in my practice. When I talk to my clients about assertive communication, I usually ask them to start small.

Begin by making a small request for something, or if there is something slightly annoying in your life, then address this, basically something that is not a particularly scary thing to confront, but more along the lines of a simple request.

In my experience, when someone is assertive and they stand up for their boundaries and needs, or they make a request assertively and confidently, then more often than not, that request is met.

Whenever a request is granted, it becomes a much less scary or intimidating thing than the requestor originally thought.

I had a client whose colleague always played their music too loud at work, and when my client had to do paperwork on their computer, she was always distracted by this music. However, the client was too passive and afraid to ask her colleague to turn the music down. She observed that nobody else was asking this individual to turn their music down, so she thought she must be the only one who was bothered by it.

In our session, we talked about assertive communication. We also talked about how making a request and asserting a need can sometimes be received better when you add an explanation. Instead of simply asking the individual to turn their music down, the request could be better received if she added why that was important to her.

For example, saying to her colleague: "Hey, I have a bunch of paperwork I need to get done, and I'm finding it difficult to concentrate with your music. Is it okay to turn it down a bit or maybe listen through headphones?"

When my client eventually did make this request, her colleague simply responded with, "Oh yeah, no problem," and that was it. It was no big deal. My client's colleague turned the music down, and other people thanked my client later because they were also distracted by the music!

This is consistent with another observation I've made, that when you're thinking something, chances are that other people are thinking about it also.

When it comes to assertive communication, adding an explanation can be very helpful. For example, if you're asking for a day off, you can simply ask for it, but if your boss knows why you want the day off, it can be easier to accommodate.

> **Assertive communication empowers you to speak up, not to dominate.**

This doesn't mean that you have to tell your personal story or give out information that you don't want to. For example, if someone asks you if you want to hang out with them on the weekend and you don't want to or you have other things to do, then you might simply say no. However, they may keep pushing you, but if you tell them you have this other thing you need to do on the weekend, they may be less likely to ask again because they know the explanation.

Going back to what I said a little bit before about my observation of people thinking the same thing, if you're afraid to ask a question, which is also relevant to assertiveness, chances are, if you're asking the question, someone else is wondering about it too.

One personal example of this was during my master's degree in mental health counseling, and in one of the classes, there was a term that came up over and over in the textbook. The teacher would use this term, and I had no idea what this counseling term was. Because I was already in the field of psychology and the counseling profession, I felt nervous asking what this term meant because I thought I would look like a complete idiot if I asked.

In my head, I assumed that this term was a very basic and common thing, and for me to be this far along in a counseling career and not even know what this meant would make me look very stupid.

Several weeks went by, and I felt like I was hindering my learning if I didn't ask. I knew I would rather know than not, so I finally got the courage to ask the teacher. What I didn't expect was that more than half of the class was so relieved that I asked this question because they also had not heard it, and they were thinking that they were stupid too!

It became very comical because as soon as I asked the question, so many of the students expressed the same thought, and we all laughed about it. So many of the students wanted to ask but didn't, for the same reason as why I had waited so long to ask!

It was from this moment on that I knew it was okay to ask questions because if you're wondering about something, somebody else is probably wondering about it too.

For example, if someone cuts in line and everyone is too passive to tell that person they cut in line, but you're the one that says to the person that you believe they cut in line and that the line starts back there, even though nobody dared to confront that person, they're all thinking the same thing and they're all relieved because you spoke up.

The experience I've had with my clients is that when I encourage them to assert themselves in a small way, then it builds confidence because, more often than not, their request is granted, and when their request is met, they feel better about asking because they've received a positive response.

This starts a snowball effect. With that increased confidence, they also become more able to ask more questions or to assert their needs. It's very cool to witness this.

In the event of my client who asked her colleague to turn the music down, she was very relieved and pleasantly surprised by how easily her request was accommodated. The colleague made no big deal about it, and my client's anxiety about asking this small thing became a much bigger deal in her mind.

Now, if a similar situation happened to her and she wanted to make another request from someone else, she would be more confident and able to bring this new issue up because her previous request was met with a positive response.

The thing I want to highlight, which is a recurring theme I have experienced with my clients, is that assertive communication is not the same as aggressive communication. It's okay to stand up for your needs, and you can do this in a way that maintains healthy communication between both parties.

It's completely appropriate to stand up for your boundaries, and adding different pieces to it, such as paying attention to your body language and portraying confidence, can help you meet those needs.

By starting small in your requests and assertiveness, especially if you are a passive communicator, you can work toward building confidence, which can make it easier to make more requests and establish boundaries in the future. You may find that asserting your boundaries and making requests is not as scary as you had assumed and that the more you experience positive responses, the easier this will become.

19
INTEGRITY

I think that integrity is one of the greatest things because I believe integrity is one of the higher moral values. Integrity doesn't involve other people; it's about being true to yourself and being honest regardless of the presence of others.

One of the more popular definitions of integrity is that integrity is doing the right thing even when no one is watching. I believe that, as humans, generally, we take shortcuts, and overall, if we can do something faster or easier, then that's the path we're inclined to take.

Maybe, in some ways, this is a good thing because things can become more efficient. When we look at this from the framework of efficiency then we look at how we can work smarter. However, from a moral perspective, taking the shortcut is not always the desired way.

Integrity is doing the right thing even when no one is watching.

I think integrity entails a few things. It involves doing the right thing, but more specifically, doing the right thing even when you're the only one who knows you're doing the right thing. I think another aspect of integrity is about being true to who you are and what you believe in.

When I talk about integrity being about being true to who you are, what I mean is being in line with your beliefs and values. If you believe in something, then that's what you honor, and you act according to your values.

Maybe the opposite of integrity is hypocrisy because hypocrisy is saying one thing but doing another, and your actions don't reflect your words. So integrity involves your actions lining up with your words, again, not in the context of other people or that other people can see, but more in the context of doing it for yourself.

I believe there are many different types of integrity. When I talk about moral integrity, I think it can branch out in many ways.

One of the ways we see hypocrisy manifest in different settings is in a religious setting. One of the more common observations that my clients experience and then talk about is encountering people who are horrible to others or very judgmental of others, yet when they go to church, they are nice to everyone. In church, they hear religious teachings but don't apply those same teachings in their lives.

These behaviors become very hypocritical because some of these same individuals preach one thing, and they have their fixed beliefs about humanity, but they don't practice what they believe in.

You see this manifest in other settings also. There are numerous cases of religious leaders who are strong in their teachings and then we come to find out that they are perpetrators of the sins they preach about.

I believe integrity is about values and beliefs and identifying what those are for you. There are things that you feel strongly about, and integrity is about following through with those values in your actions as well as your words.

For example, say someone believes in compassion and helping

others. Well, integrity would entail that this person can demonstrate this value in their actions. They would be compassionate toward humankind. They would follow through with what they believe in, and the action of helping others becomes a reflection of their values.

Maybe this person ends up volunteering or becomes part of a charity, not because this looks good from a societal point of view, and not so that other people can say what an amazing person they are, but genuinely because this is what they believe in.

They are not driven by external feedback for their positive behaviors. The motivation does not come from recognition by others, or other people speaking highly of them because they are doing good work, or the societal response. Integrity comes from an internal motivation. It comes from their belief that helping is good, and therefore, doing volunteer work and charity work is good.

Integrity comes from internal feedback, and because they have their values, ultimately, this is the motivating factor; it's all that matters. So when they go out there and do good work, they could be the only person who knows about it, but that's okay because they're following their integrity rather than an external reward.

This is one of the highest moral ideals because only then are you in line with your values and your beliefs.

In my work as a counselor, I always strive for professional integrity. Many aspects of counseling add to professional integrity, such as confidentiality, correct billing, and being present with my clients, and I strive to always maintain integrity in my practice.

You can cut corners on things and try to find the shortcuts, or you can try to do things the easy way with whatever your job responsibilities are, but I think that when it comes to professional integrity, you can choose to do it the right way.

Doing something the right way may take you longer, but one thing that I have observed repeatedly is that the feeling of satisfaction is going to be a lot greater because of applying integrity.

When you do something right, it feels better. There's a deeper sense of satisfaction that is present, and this, in turn, stimulates the internal reward system.

> Notice what you complain about,
> it might be the very thing
> you need to address within yourself.

Integrity is in the realm of responsibilities. Integrity is about doing a job well and doing a job thoroughly. Integrity is about saying what you're going to do and doing what you believe in. It's about following through and showing that your actions match your words. It's about being motivated by your values rather than an external reward.

For example, I want to do my job well in the counseling profession and maintain professional integrity, not because I want everyone to tell me how great a counselor I am, which is great when it happens, but because I want to know for myself that I'm doing the right thing. I want to know for myself that I did the best I could and that I'm following the ethical guidelines.

Another area where professional integrity manifests is with finances. I use a credit card processing system, and I remember one time when I accidentally entered the wrong number, and I charged a client ten cents too much. The client blew it off, saying it was only ten cents and not to worry about it, but I insisted that she be reimbursed this amount. It doesn't matter if the error is on a small scale or a large scale, but doing what I know is right.

Integrity is also about following through on your words. If I say I'm going to do something, then I'm going to do my best to follow through with that thing. I believe this is also applicable to professional integrity in addition to personal integrity.

Professional integrity is about the mission statement and the core values that drive your career, whatever that career may be. For example, the medical profession has the Hippocratic oath, and in the counseling profession, this is the Code of Ethics. Professional integrity is about adhering to values and ensuring they are followed. It's not about fear of losing your job or being monitored, but about honestly knowing you did the right thing.

Integrity works on so many different levels. It also manifests within interpersonal relationships. Within a relationship, are you who you say you are, or do you present yourself differently?

I don't ask that question in a malicious sense, per se. We all present somewhat differently depending on who we're with, and we show different sides of ourselves when we're with different people because we relate differently to different people.

You're probably a different person with your mom than with your friends, your colleagues, or your boss. This is human nature, and there's nothing malicious about that. What I'm referring to is more about whether you're presenting yourself in a way that isn't in line with your values.

Maybe there's even room for exploration here. If your actions don't line up with your words or intentions, and you feel like certain aspects of your life don't line up with your values, then maybe this is something to explore.

By exploring why your actions are different or why you act differently with different people, you may learn more about yourself and your values, which can lead to greater integrity.

One of the concepts in counseling that originated from Carl Jung is the concept of the shadow. The shadow he refers to is about the parts of ourselves that we want to keep hidden, but it can also be the part of ourselves that complains the loudest. It represents the negative aspects of ourselves and the negative parts that we don't like about ourselves. The shadow is about those parts of ourselves that we don't want others to see.

We sometimes stop dealing with our shadow because we see it as a negative part of our lives. However, there's a whole lot of learning and insight to be gained from confronting. One thing is clear: facing our shadow leads to personal growth. I saw this also when I first learned about this concept, and at first, I was very skeptical because it didn't make sense to me, but I was surprised that it is so.

The consistent thing is this. People who repeatedly complain about something tend to have that same flaw in themselves. When I first learned about this, I thought this didn't make any sense because it seemed to me a contradiction. I thought it would be the people who are opposite to this who would be the ones complaining, and the reason they complain is specifically that they're not like that, but in my observation, this is not the case.

It's a very interesting observation to make. For example, people who can be mean, aloof, distant, or standoffish type individuals are often the first to complain about other people who are standoffish, not realizing that they are exactly like that!

It sounds incredibly hypocritical, but I've observed time and time again that the people who complain about things themselves are the people they complain about!

If you want to increase integrity in your life, maybe one place to start looking is at your complaints. The things you judge others for could be a clue for you to identify that whatever it is you're complaining about, you may be lacking in yourself.

For example, if you tend to complain about people who are constantly negative, then this may be something to explore within yourself. Are you yourself a negative individual?

To increase integrity, instead of complaining about people who are negative, focus on becoming more positive yourself and finding the positives in others before judging them. You can take this experience and learn from it. You can identify the thing that you repeatedly complain about and begin turning this around. You can make an intentional decision, a conscious effort to be more positive toward others. You may make an intention to practice more kindness toward others because now you practice with greater integrity.

The interesting fallacy that happens is that when you start practicing more kindness toward others, and you're bridging the gap of hypocrisy and leaning toward integrity, then you probably even find that you don't complain about others as much! This is because you begin to change your perspective of others and work toward seeing the kindness in others more, as you bring out your kindness more.

In my experience, integrity is not something we talk about a lot, but I feel like it's an important thing. For example, in a career, it would be important to be in a job that is in line with your values. Are you chasing money while you're doing a job you hate or don't believe in? Where is the integrity in that?

You can then identify that materially, you're very well off, but what does this do for you psychologically or emotionally? You may be burning yourself out. You're setting yourself up for negative experiences about your job, and eventually, the job may not work out anyway because you don't have integrity within that job.

The same thing applies to relationships. If you're with someone and the person you're with isn't in line with your values, you're going to become increasingly dissatisfied in your relationship.

One of the ways to tell if integrity is not a part of your life is whether there is unhappiness there. There would be internal conflict because you're not in line with your beliefs and values. If part of your value system is being kind and compassionate to others, and the person you are with is rather selfish, then this will create a lot of internal conflict. The integrity of your values isn't there because you've aligned yourself with someone who doesn't align with your values.

I would challenge you, the reader, to explore in what ways you are and are not practicing integrity in your life. If you find that you're not, then explore what those areas of your life are. The way to identify if you're not practicing integrity in different areas of your life is to identify in what ways you feel like a hypocrite.

Do you complain about others when you are guilty of that same thing? Are you trying to take shortcuts and do things the easy way? Do your words say one thing, but your actions show something else?

Take, for example, a health guru who promotes healthy food and provides healthy recipes, but they eat very crappy foods when they're by themselves.

The thing about integrity is that whatever value you're maintaining integrity about, it's only important for you. It's not important for anybody else, only for you. So I challenge you to think about that. You can do whatever you want to do on your own. If nobody is watching or monitoring you, then there are no consequences. However, I encourage you to practice integrity for yourself. Notice the increased personal satisfaction you feel as a result of practicing and maintaining integrity.

In my journey, professional integrity has been very important to me. One example of this is that I used to work at a community mental health agency (the same one I have already talked about in this book), and this was when I was in the process of applying for the Assistant Behavioral Health Director position.

I ended up accepting a contract in corrections and stayed on with the community mental health agency in a part-time capacity. After a few years, the culture of the mental health agency changed. When I was first hired on with them, they were all about helping clients, but as the company grew and grew, I began to observe a lesser priority on serving clients and a higher priority on growing and revenue.

I felt like the culture was no longer about helping others, and it felt too much like a business. Several other factors ultimately made me decide to leave this agency and focus on my corrections contract and self-employed private practice.

When I put my notice in, I talked to several staff members about my reasons. We discussed the culture change that was felt by many of the staff there, and one of these colleagues had been on the interview panel when I applied for the Assistant Behavioral Health Director position. One of the things she told me, and I had forgotten that I had even answered the question in this way, was that one of the questions in my interview from years before was whether I would be committed to the Assistant Behavioral Health Director position, and could the agency rely on me being there long-term?

I don't even remember being asked the question, but she told me that my response was that as long as the agency's values were in line with my values, I would stay on with them. She thought that it was interesting that several years later, I chose to put in my notice for this very reason.

I also found it interesting that my answer from years before was still in line with my decision to leave the agency, showing the consistency of my values.

This is what I mean when I talk about professional integrity. When your job is in line with your values, then you increase job satisfaction because it feels right. When you live a life in accordance with your personal values, you increase your sense of personal satisfaction as well.

20
PHYSICAL SELF-CARE

In this chapter, I want to highlight the importance of self-care. This is a recurring theme in counseling because I believe it builds the foundation for a lot of things.

Maslow's Hierarchy of Needs highlights that you have to have certain things in place before you can address other things. For example, the bottom of the pyramid outlined in Maslow's Hierarchy of Needs shows the foundational things we need, such as food, shelter, warmth, etc., and it doesn't become productive to address the higher needs, such as psychological needs or spiritual/existential questions if those base needs are not met.

I saw this manifest a lot in community mental health, where many of the clients were more in crisis mode. Counseling was sometimes more about putting out fires. It was a lot more challenging to get into the therapeutic aspects of their lives because they were often experiencing a housing crisis, or their children were involved with child protective services.

Sometimes, they had legal issues they were dealing with, or they were regulars at the food bank because they didn't have enough money for food for the month.

With these circumstances in place, it was challenging to address traumas or explore emotions when they were worrying about how to pay next month's rent.

Similarly, basic physical self-care is fundamental to psychological or emotional care. I talk about physical self-care a lot with my clients because if the foundation of physical self-care is not present, then I can only do so much. For example, if a client is chronically sleep-deprived and they are not making sleep a priority, it's going to be very challenging to address their moods and emotional volatility, their inability to focus and concentrate, because a lot of those things are dependent on good sleep, not on good coping skills.

Self-care builds the foundation for emotional and psychological wellness.

The same goes for nutrition, hydration, or other basic physical needs. So, the topic of self-care becomes very important to mental health because there are a lot of different aspects of self-care that are closely linked to psychological issues.

For example, depression. Symptoms of depression include lack of motivation, low energy, things that are fun are not appealing anymore (also called anhedonia), irritability, a low mood, and low stress tolerance. A lot of these symptoms will manifest when many aspects of self-care are not happening, sleep deprivation being one of them.

If you take a healthy, high-functioning individual who has no history of mental health issues, and you cut their sleep by an hour every night, and you make them slightly more sleep-deprived, you're going to see all sorts of issues emerge. These include many of the same symptoms of depression that I described above, like inability to focus, low energy and motivation, irritability, etc.

Self-care is so important to mental health. For example, if you have someone who experiences high anxiety but then you find out they are drinking ten cups of coffee every day, then looking into changing physical habits is more effective than looking at anxiety coping skills. I can tell you right now that if I drank ten cups of coffee every day, I'd be a mess!

When I talk about physical self-care in sessions, I also talk about ruling out physical causes of different presenting problems. For example, thyroid issues can be very common, and a lot of people experience these. An underactive thyroid mimics many of the same symptoms as depression, whereas an overactive thyroid mimics a lot of the same symptoms as anxiety.

If you come into a counseling session and you haven't had a wellness check in a long time, then I would start there because it's always good to rule out physical causes for mental health issues.

There are numerous aspects of self-care that I believe are important. First, there is the wellness check to see if everything is healthy physically. This includes basic lab work and whatever else a doctor will recommend to you.

In addition to thyroid functioning issues, other issues, such as low blood sugar, can increase emotional volatility, so it's always important to rule out medical causes.

I recently had a client who complained of low motivation, irritability, low energy, and lethargy. She rated fairly high on the scale for depression. She was encouraged to get a wellness check as she hadn't been to the doctor in a while, and when her lab results came back, she was highly anemic. There are many ways we could have addressed symptoms of depression in therapy, but countering symptoms of anemia would be very hard indeed.

The realm of physical self-care to manage emotional self-care is such a huge topic that I believe this could be a book in itself. However, I want to highlight some of the recurring conversations I have with my clients about self-care, as this is fundamental to emotional wellness.

Other aspects of self-care that become important to emotional wellness are sleep and nutrition. I am not a nutritionist or dietitian and would never give dietary advice, but I do believe that clients know from a common sense perspective what is healthy for them and what isn't.

I remember a long time ago, in my beginning days as a counselor, I had a client who told me that she was feeling anxious. She had low motivation and was often lethargic. She stated that she sometimes felt light-headed, so we explored coping skills to manage anxiety.

After a while, I asked her about self-care and nutrition, and she responded with "chicken and rice." I assumed chicken and rice for dinner, which she confirmed, so I asked her what her other meals looked like. She again responded with "chicken and rice." Lunch was chicken and rice. Breakfast was chicken and rice. All she ate throughout her entire day, every day, was chicken and rice!

I had to ask her several times to clarify that this was not a misunderstanding, but no, all she ate was chicken and rice. She never ate any fruits or vegetables, only chicken and rice every single day.

I'm no expert in nutrition, but I'm willing to guess that if I only ate chicken and rice every single day, I probably would end up feeling some effects from being deprived of other nutrients.

I encouraged this client to explore ways to increase her variety of foods and possibly even work with a nutritionist to help in this aspect of her life, as I was sure that several of her symptoms that manifested as emotional needs were due to nutrition issues.

Some things are common knowledge when it comes to the way different substances affect us and how different substances cause different emotional states. Too much sugar creates hyperactivity. Unfortunately, a lot of children eat breakfast with a very high sugar content, including children diagnosed with ADHD (attention deficit hyperactivity disorder). Pop-Tarts, orange juice, and cereals are all loaded with sugar, and this is a staple breakfast for some. No wonder these children are fidgety, and they have difficulty concentrating!

Alcohol is another substance that alters mood. Many people believe that alcohol is an instant mood changer and that the effects of alcohol are only experienced while intoxicated. However, I have seen in my clients an increase in general anxiety throughout their day, with increased alcohol intake. These same clients report back that their anxiety levels decrease when alcohol intake decreases.

One thing that alcohol does is decrease the quality of sleep. You may sleep the same number of hours, but when you drink alcohol before bed, it doesn't allow you to go into the deeper and more restorative stages of sleep. You will experience the signs of sleep deprivation, such as increased irritability.

Another self-care factor that affects mental health is medication. If a client is taking psychotropic medication, then it becomes important to see if they are consistent with their medication or if they are having issues with their medication. It is always important to encourage clients to keep the lines of communication with their prescriber open and for them to always make medication changes under the supervision of their prescriber.

Even vitamins can be a discussion. For example, in northern countries and US states, vitamin D deficiency is prevalent because the sun doesn't provide enough vitamin D in the winter months. Some of the symptoms of a vitamin D deficiency also mimic some symptoms of depression, such as low mood, fatigue, and feeling weak.

Say, for example, you live a pretty high-stress life. You have a lot of responsibilities, and you work. You have children, and you're also working on several projects. In addition, you're trying to coordinate your children's extracurricular activities, and for you, life is always about being on the go. Maybe in those circumstances, you would already be prone to stress because of the nature of your lifestyle.

However, if you take away some of the physical self-care aspects, your entire ability to manage that level of stress is going to change dramatically.

Say you take two individuals with the same stress levels. They both have the same high-demanding job, and they have the same number of responsibilities outside of work. They have similar family lives and are juggling several responsibilities at a time.

> **Two people can have the same stress level but drastically different resiliency based on self-care.**

Now, say that one of these individuals does a good job taking care of themselves. They eat healthy and stay hydrated, and they make sleep a priority. If they take medication, they take it consistently and as prescribed. They have a healthy social network and healthy coping skills.

The other person, however, has the same responsibilities, but instead of taking care of themselves, they stay up late and have a few drinks every night before they go to bed. They go to bed later because they browse social media before going to sleep, so their brain is stimulated when they close their eyes.

Because of these poor sleep habits, they feel more tired and, therefore, less motivated when they wake up, so they grab something quick and easy to eat instead of taking time to prepare something healthier. Throughout the day, because they had a Pop-Tart for breakfast, they feel hungry before lunch, so they may eat a heavier lunch, which causes them to crash throughout the afternoon, causing them to want to drink more caffeine and sugar.

By the time they come home from work, they're tired. They have more difficulty focusing because of sleep deprivation. In the evening, their energy level is lower, so they neglect the projects they want to work on in the evening. And because of this fatigue, they may be more inclined to turn to alcohol to cope with this increased stress and fatigue. This is the ripple effect of neglecting self-care.

Healthier individuals prioritize sleep. They wake up more refreshed and motivated to prepare a healthier breakfast before they go to work. Because of this healthier nutrition, they can focus a little better throughout their day, which means that they become more conscientious with their lunch choice, which sets them up for better concentration in the afternoon.

Now, when these healthier individuals get home from work, and they want to work on some projects, they have the energy to work on those. They go to bed feeling more emotionally satisfied because they were able to work on some personal projects outside of work.

Their overall ability to manage their day has improved because of nothing other than self-care habits. The difference in resiliency levels between these two individuals had nothing to do with coping skills or psychological factors. The only difference was how they took care of themselves.

Another important self-care aspect that affects emotional wellness is social wellness. Having a positive support system and having friends is so important. Ultimately, we're social creatures. We're not designed to be isolated. As I'm writing this book on the tail end of the COVID-19 pandemic, I can say with certainty that people's mental health has been compromised by the pandemic and increased isolation. In addition to being isolated from friends and social interactions because of social distancing, working from home has affected many people.

A lot of people have been feeling isolated because they have had to work from home, and they've been cut off from society in general. As a counselor, I know that I'm busier and more in demand than I have ever been before. The feedback that I'm receiving from clients who are seeking services is that it's almost impossible to find a counselor because everyone is full.

There are a lot of layers and aspects of stress around the pandemic that have affected mental health, but in addition to the fear of contracting COVID-19, the effects of social isolation have been a huge factor in declining mental health.

People who have friends, who have people they can connect with, tend to do a lot better. People who have solid family support systems do a lot better. The same goes for individuals who struggle with addiction and are working on recovery. One of the biggest contributing factors to individuals who successfully recover from addiction is that they have a good support system.

People who go through significant major life events, for example, grief and loss or illness, tend to get through these major life stressors with the help of positive family and friends.

Social wellness is huge, and social wellness also has a ripple effect. When you don't take care of yourself, and you're feeling worse, you have a greater tendency to want to isolate. Now you want to remove yourself from the world, and maybe your friends start fading away, or they start keeping their distance because you're never interested in doing what they want to do anyway.

The lack of social support and increased isolation increase those negative feelings and depression, which in turn increases the tendency to want to isolate. So now you end up in a loop that can make mental health symptoms worse.

One of the aspects of self-care that is a recurring theme in my counseling sessions is identifying a social support network. This could be through family or friends, or through increasing connections with colleagues. This could also be about getting involved in groups that are meaningful to them. This could be through church or a fitness group, but whatever this looks like, it's about increasing connection with others.

In the documentary "Happy," they talk about three intrinsic and three extrinsic values that are perceived to contribute to happiness. The extrinsic values, such as money and image, end up creating more stress. However, the three intrinsic factors that contribute to happiness are personal growth, contribution, and connection with others.

We simply do a lot better when we connect with others. If you tend to isolate, I challenge you to find at least some meaningful connection to others. Connection is not about engaging in big social gatherings and having an extensive network of friends, because this can be exhausting and daunting. Sometimes, having even only one or two meaningful people in our lives can make a huge difference in how we cope with negative emotions.

Social wellness is a big part of psychological wellness.

Another self-care aspect that influences psychological and emotional wellness is fitness and exercise. And when I say fitness and exercise, what I'm talking about is movement.

Movement is about getting your heart rate up, and this can be done in so many ways. What happens when you move and get your heart rate up is that you're increasing the endorphin, dopamine, and serotonin levels in your body. These are the chemicals in our body that affect motivation levels, regulate emotions, and improve mood.

When runners talk about the "runner's high," this is what they are experiencing. A lot of people struggle with getting their workout started, but when they're done, they feel great! This is because of an increase in the feel-good chemicals in the body!

It's simply a biochemical response in the brain, but a change in these chemicals changes how we feel. When we work out, we're changing the biochemistry in our brains, and we're increasing the antidepressants that are already naturally within us.

When people have low levels of serotonin in the brain, this is when symptoms of depression manifest. Many antidepressants change serotonin levels in the brain, but when you raise serotonin levels in your brain naturally from movement and exercise, then what that means is that exercising is not *like* an antidepressant; it *is* an antidepressant.

The same ripple effect that social interaction has is also present with increasing exercise. If you experience low energy, then you may experience lower levels of the feel-good chemicals in your brain. Because of the lower energy and mood, you may tend not to exercise because this requires a certain energy level to get up and moving. However, if you do start moving and begin increasing the natural feel-good chemicals in your brain, you begin to improve your mood and increase your energy levels, and this makes it easier to continue with exercise.

If you want to start taking more control over feeling better, you want to experience increased energy levels, and you feel you want to resolve some mental health issues, e.g., trauma, grief, or anger, but you don't know where to start, one good place to start to build a foundation is by starting with your self-care.

I would also say that out of all the different aspects of self-care, one of the biggest ones to focus on is sleep. If there is only one thing you can prioritize to make yourself feel better, start by managing your sleep.

There is a lot of information already out there about good sleep hygiene practices, but here are a few key things to do and not do if you want to experience good sleep.

One change is not to use electronics late at night. Even though we think we're relaxing when we're watching a movie or so, our bodies are relaxing, but our brains are getting fired up and stimulated, which is not going to help our ability to mentally wind down when we close our eyes.

Alcohol decreases the quality of sleep because, with alcohol consumption, you don't reach the deeper and more restorative phases of sleep.

Going to bed on time to make sure you get the right number of hours is also important. This can be an issue for a lot of people, especially if you have a lot of responsibilities and always need more hours in the day.

There is a term called "revenge bedtime procrastination" that refers to the tendency to stay up late to do things entertaining or relaxing (like scrolling social media!) because of the feeling of being robbed of this throughout the day, yet this is done at the expense of sleep.

Reading before bed can be helpful because it makes your eyes tired, and it doesn't stimulate your brain like screen time does.

Creating a nighttime routine is also helpful because we're creatures of habit, and when we do the same thing every day, we start to condition our bodies to get used to anticipating what to expect. So, when you create the same nighttime routine every night, you're training and conditioning your body to start winding down.

Of course, limiting caffeine and sugar is hopefully one of the more obvious healthy habits, too! There are a lot more tips for good sleep, but these are some of the more common habits.

People who have known me in the past may consider me very hypocritical. I'm talking about good sleep hygiene because I used to be very chronically sleep-deprived. I'm naturally more of a night owl, and even though I had to wake up very early for work, I would still stay up late. I did notice firsthand the unhealthy ripple effect that this had, however, and once I transitioned to full-time private practice, I was able to adjust my work schedule to better suit my circadian rhythm and accommodate more sleep.

When you're in a pattern of sleep deprivation, then lethargy and dredging through your day become your norm. This may become what you expect normal to feel like, but when you work on improving sleep, you may be surprised at the changes you experience. If you are chronically sleep-deprived, then you don't know what you're missing until you experience it. This was certainly the case for me.

I felt like I was functioning well, and I was still managing my many different responsibilities. However, it wasn't until I improved my sleep that I realized that I was functioning nowhere near capacity. Now that I'm sleeping better, I can look back and realize how exhausted I was. Being sleep-deprived was a baseline for me, and that was what I perceived to be normal.

What I want to convey in this chapter is the importance of taking care of yourself. If you want to work on your mental health but you're not taking care of yourself physically, then you are limiting my capacity to help you.

It's not fair to feed your children Pop-Tarts, chocolate cereal, and orange juice for breakfast and then ask them to sit still and concentrate. It's a losing battle! If you want to concentrate better but you're drinking ten cups of coffee, then I can teach you all the skills, but they're not likely to work because your physical habits are getting in the way. If you have low thyroid functioning, then I can teach you all the depression coping skills, but they're not likely to work because what you need is medication.

If you're not taking care of your body, you're limiting what therapy can do.

If you want to engage in emotional wellness and you want to take more control over your mental health, then physical self-care has to be a part of this. You cannot have a mentally healthy individual who doesn't take care of themselves in any way. You cannot have a chronically sleep-deprived and emotionally healthy individual.

Mental health symptoms are going to be easier to manage, and resilience levels go up. Stress tolerance increases, and your ability to take on the day becomes easier. Mood stability increases, and all of this happens when you focus on improving self-care.

21

EVERY ACTION SERVES A NEED

Something that has frequently come up, not only in individual counseling but also group counseling, especially in the prison system, is looking at the reasons and the motives for people's behavior.

This is about being able to look past the behavior to be able to identify the need. Then, you can learn from that experience and find healthier ways to function.

With this chapter, I want to write about the idea that every single behavior and everything that we do meets a need; otherwise, we wouldn't do it. If I choose to make lunch, it's because I'm hungry, or if I get into my car, it's because I have somewhere to go. Everything we do serves some kind of function, and this is relevant to all the things we do, no matter how big or small.

Even those big, significant decisions meet needs. When those needs are met positively, then that's a best-case scenario. I want to put money aside because I want to save for something in the future. So, I'm going to refrain from having something in the present so that I can benefit from having this thing in my future.

There are so many ways that our behaviors can be explained. I might eat only certain types of foods because I want to be healthier. My behavior can be explained because it meets a need. I can choose to cut my calorie intake to lose weight. My behavior is explained because it meets a need.

The interesting and sometimes confusing thing is when we get into behaviors that are negative or destructive. This can be self-destructive behaviors or aggressive behaviors toward others. I want to talk about this because this does come up in counseling, and it is important to identify the need for such behaviors.

If you're engaging in a destructive behavior, the first thing to ask yourself is, what need is this behavior fulfilling? For example, if you hurt someone else, it could be because you're very angry at that moment, and you're lashing out. The immediate need that this behavior fulfills is a release of tension that the anger has created.

What served you in survival mode
may sabotage you in thriving mode.

If someone engages in self-harm behaviors, this is, of course, incredibly destructive. However, even this destructive self-harm behavior meets a need. An individual would not be engaging in self-harm behaviors if it didn't meet a need. Often, the need that is being met when someone engages in self-harm behaviors is a release of tension.

A lot of times, when people engage in destructive behavior, they are usually meeting an *immediate* need. In sessions, I often talk about immediate versus delayed/deferred gratification because sometimes we have to give up what we want now to get what we want later. This is deferred gratification.

For example, if I want to lose weight, then I cannot eat all this delicious food today, but if I don't eat all this delicious food now, then I'm going to feel much better about myself later. I have to give up what I want now to get what I want later.

I would argue that most of the time, when there are destructive or impulsive behaviors present, the need that is being met is in the realm of immediate gratification. It's meeting a need now.

A lot of times, when an immediate gratification need is being met, it also means that the long-term gratification is being compromised. For example, if I want to eat this awful food right now, then it might taste amazing right now, and I'm going to enjoy it now. However, I'm compromising my weight loss in the future, and if I keep up with those unhealthy habits, then I'm never going to be able to lose weight in the future.

Another example is if I'm saving up for a new car or something significant. But then I go into a store and see those shoes and think, wow, those shoes are amazing! I want to buy those shoes! I'm meeting my immediate gratification need by buying shoes that look good right now and that make me feel good right now. However, I'm compromising my long-term goal of being able to buy a car.

Behaviors are always motivated by meeting a need. The need is either in the realm of long-term or short-term gratification. When we meet the long-term need instead of the short-term and go in line with deferred gratification instead of immediate gratification, this is usually the more satisfying of the two because this follows the long-term happiness, the satisfaction, the contentment.

When we meet the need for immediate gratification, then this is usually more of a short-term feel-good feeling, like an impulse buy. We think this new thing we bought is awesome, but maybe a week later, we don't care. Or the food we eat tastes amazing at the moment, but half an hour later, the taste is gone, and that experience is gone.

I also believe that, as humans, we lean toward immediate gratification. We're very much wired to receive rewards now and worry about the aftermath later. This is especially true if the consequences of our choices don't manifest right at the decision-making moment but instead are delayed.

For example, there are so many significant health issues that go along with smoking, but because those health issues don't manifest today, we don't worry about them. It's the same with eating unhealthy foods. This delicious but awful-for-me meal that I eat today is not going to affect me today, but if I keep doing this, I will experience health issues in the future.

Now imagine that these health issues showed up the minute after you ate that unhealthy food or the minute after you smoked the cigarette. Nobody would be smoking, and everyone would be eating healthy! But unfortunately, that's not how that works!

Going back to identifying the need for behaviors, if you have someone who is in a repetitive pattern of negative behaviors, you may start by encouraging that person to stop the behaviors because it's not healthy. Well, chances are this has crossed their minds! Whoever engages in negative and unhealthy behaviors already knows they are, and this advice is not particularly helpful. Negative behaviors, especially repetitive ones, are not always easy to redirect.

One approach to address this, and this is an avenue I explore with my clients, is to identify what the individual is getting out of making those choices. What needs are being met through those behaviors?

Changing your behavior isn't about trying harder; it's about getting your needs met differently.

For example, say I have a client who tends to drink a lot in the evenings, maybe not too much that everything is compromised, but enough to be concerned, to be disappointed in themselves, to wake up feeling unrested, and to continue craving alcohol every day. Their alcohol intake could still be affecting them psychologically because they are still engaging in unwanted repetitive behavior.

The client comes to my office feeling inner conflict and disappointment in themselves. They are continuing a behavior they don't want but can't seem to stop.

We can take the approach of changing their choices and exploring what they need to do to stop drinking. We can explore things they can do instead of drinking, and this may be productive on some level, but this doesn't necessarily change the behavior because they've likely thought of that already! The reason they're in my session is precisely because they're continuing with a behavior that they don't want to be doing.

The missing piece with the above-mentioned approach is that we have not explored what need is being met through alcohol intake. It could be several different things. For example, they believe that drinking alcohol could be a way to relax at night. Maybe when they come home from work, and they've had a long and stressful day, they feel they need to unwind from everything. The need that alcohol intake meets is stress relief.

Another need that alcohol intake could be meeting is a way to numb emotions. Maybe they are dealing with inner disappointments, which could be feeding feelings of inadequacy, which then creates more cravings for alcohol, which in turn creates the need to numb these uncomfortable emotions, and now we're in a vicious cycle.

The need for alcohol could also stem from unresolved emotions that stem from way back, and alcohol is a way to keep them from having to deal with the past.

When you identify the need you're meeting with your behavior, then you've reached the first step. Once you've identified the need, the second step is to identify how you can fulfill that same need more healthily.

For example, if you identify that drinking every night is about stress relief, then this is the need you're meeting. Now, you can focus on identifying ways to reduce stress in healthier ways or how to better manage stress.

Now, you can work on identifying all the factors in your life that are contributing to stress. You can work on identifying what you can maybe change in your life to help reduce that stress. What are you taking on in your life that you don't necessarily need to? Are you saying yes to too many things? Are there things in your life that you can drop to free up some more time?

The other way to address this issue is to focus not on reducing stress in life but also on finding healthier stress-coping skills. If the person who drinks a lot of alcohol wants to keep the same number of responsibilities in their life, what are some healthier stress-coping strategies that they can implement so that they can still feel stress relief, but not through alcohol?

So now, instead of focusing on ways to change the behavior, the focus turns to stress management because you've identified the causes and the reasons behind the behavior.

When it comes to more internal processes that are at the root of behaviors, such as feelings of inadequacy, disappointment in yourself, not feeling worthy or deserving, or emotional conflicts that you're dealing with, then usually the need that alcohol is meeting is numbing those emotions. The need that alcohol is meeting is so that the individual doesn't have to feel these emotions or deal with these emotions. This is meeting the immediate gratification need of the situation.

The way to meet this need in the long-term gratification realm is to address the trauma and work on clearing this out for good.

For example, if feelings of inadequacy or unworthiness stem from childhood trauma, then this is what needs to be processed. Identifying the underlying factors that are causing these types of emotions makes it possible to address them.

If you take someone who has an anger problem and acting out aggressively provides a release of tension for them, then you can approach this two-fold. First, what are some different ways they can manage their anger, and what different outlets can they utilize for their anger that are not as destructive? For example, when this individual is feeling angry or frustrated, then maybe they could go for a run, engage in physical activity, or apply mindful breathing skills.

Second, what is causing this anger in the first place? The approach is to address the actual root causes of the anger and what the individual is responding to. Find out what is being triggered in that individual to provoke this response. Find ways to resolve these underlying issues so that anger is not as prevalent in the first place.

Anger management can involve exploring the individual's expectations of others and helping reframe their thoughts, so anger doesn't arise as frequently. Many times, anger is about unmet expectations, so reframing anger is about how you can continue to feel good despite not having your expectations met.

One of the ways to help resolve destructive behaviors is to first identify the need behind the behavior and, second, how you address this need in healthier ways.

Another recurring thing in counseling sessions is the question of whether the identified needs are being met. For example, I had a client who had a lot of anger issues, and this was a learned behavior. She learned throughout her life that she needed to protect her emotions, and she only knew how to do this by being angry. Everyone in her life had not been safe for her, and she then went on to learn that when she was the aggressor, she was safer because she kept others at a distance.

This anger became a meaningful behavior, and it served a purpose. Her aggressive behavior was meeting a need; however, her aggression was no longer useful in the present, but now she was stuck in this pattern of behavior because she had become so used to it.

My client was still very reactive and aggressive, even though it no longer met her needs. It had now become a learned behavior because it had been meaningful at some point in the past.

This is an important factor to consider. It's important to identify what needs a behavior meets, but it's also important to look at what needs that behavior possibly served in the past that might not be relevant anymore.

For example, this could apply to people with addictive behaviors or when people engage in behaviors because they're simply habits. Those behaviors may have met a need at some time in the past, but they don't serve this need anymore. However, now they're stuck in the pattern of those behaviors.

If the current unhealthy behavior is not meeting a need anymore, then that behavior needs to change. This could involve exploring what past needs were being met and working on resolving that, in addition to helping the client practice different ways of responding and utilizing healthier coping skills and outlets for difficult emotions.

If you're engaged in destructive behavior and you want to change that behavior, then maybe one of the most important things to identify first is not only to focus on changing the behavior, which is usually the default response, but to go deeper and identify what the need behind the behavior is.

A very common behavior that a lot of people want to change is their eating habits. People want to change their weight by altering their eating and workout routines, and the approach many people take is that they know they need to eat healthier, so they know what they need to change.

They usually then set a start date and set an intention that on that date, they are going to start eating healthier. But then, a few days later, they give up and resort to old eating habits. What they haven't done is to explore why, when they are engaging in those unhealthy eating habits, what need the behavior is meeting.

Are you eating unhealthily because it provides comfort from stress? If that is the identified need, then the approach has to be about how to better manage stress and what are some healthier alternatives to feel comfort from stress?

When you begin to explore the reasons for stress, is it because you're taking on too many responsibilities? Or are you providing comfort to cover feelings of loneliness or emptiness? If those are some of the reasons why you engage in comfort eating, then it's a lot more productive to address these underlying issues rather than simply attempting to change your eating habits only.

Are you eating unhealthily because it's quicker and easier than preparing food? Is it too much work and too time-consuming for your schedule to prepare healthy meals? If so, then the time factor hasn't been considered. If this is the need that has to be met, then you can ask yourself how you can eat food that is fast, quick, and easy but still healthy. You now problem-solve differently because you are considering your unmet needs.

Some resolution to this could be meal prepping so that you don't have to spend as much time in the kitchen preparing dinner after work. You could even consider signing up for a meal delivery service, or you could revise the types of meals you eat, from the more complicated ones to meals that use some staple foods that are easy and quick to put together.

The same thing applies to fitness. This is one of the most common things that people struggle to stay consistent with after they have decided to start. When you're not working out and keeping up with exercise, what need does this meet? Maybe it's again a time factor, where you don't feel you can fit exercise into your routine because you keep so busy.

If this is the case, now you can consider how you might be able to include exercise into your busy day while still considering the time constraints. Maybe there are ways you can incorporate fitness into your already existing workday instead of adding it to your workday. Are you able to cycle or walk to work? Can you walk during a lunch break? Can you walk to the fifth floor of your building instead of taking the elevator?

You may identify that the reason you don't go to the gym is because you feel intimidated, because you have no idea what you're doing and everyone there looks like a bodybuilder. If you identify that the need for not going is that you don't have to deal with your discomfort and insecurity about the gym, then now you can look at alternatives that consider this need.

You could maybe go to a workout class so that you have some guidance on what to do. This way, you have a facilitator who can help you when you're unsure. Or maybe you can collaborate on going to the gym with a friend so that a shared experience may not feel as intimidating and could even add fun. Or maybe you now consider more solitary exercises like running or following a fitness video online in the comfort of your own home.

Maybe you've identified that the reason you don't work out is that you lack motivation. What are some of the factors that are causing your motivation levels to be low? Is it because you're sleep-deprived? Is it because your workdays are so long that by the time you finish your workday, you're exhausted? Is it because you're being pulled in so many different directions and have too many responsibilities? Now these can be considered in your problem-solving.

There are so many different reasons why people don't work out, so when you can identify what your reasons are, only then are you going to be able to brainstorm ways you can meet those same needs and still problem-solve how to work out while meeting those needs.

The most successful way to change repetitive yet unwanted behaviors is not to rely on your conviction that you're going to change the way you do something. It's not about setting an intention and doing this because this usually doesn't last. No, changing negative behavior is about doing something more healthily while making sure your underlying needs are still being met.

22
CHOICE VS. MISTAKE

One of the things I see a lot is how the language people use changes the connotation of what they are saying, and this could be intentional or not. Within this context, I would like to talk about the distinction between a choice and a mistake, as the connotations attached to these words are very different.

This language was particularly prevalent in the prison system when I was running groups there. Often, when the inmates talked about their crimes, they would refer to them as the mistakes they made.

I would like to clarify the differences between a choice and a mistake. I believe that the biggest distinction between these two is the element of intention behind the action.

An intention behind something can clarify the meaning behind words because sometimes, different words can have similar meanings; the intention behind it gives it either a positive or a negative connotation.

An example I can think of to highlight this is the words "positive reinforcement" and "pro-social manipulation." The actions look the same. Both actions have a version of "if you do this, then I'll do this" that is present.

However, the intention behind positive reinforcement is to teach discipline, limit setting, and shape behavior; it benefits the individual on the receiving end of the positive reinforcement.

Pro-social manipulation, on the other hand, is motivated by personal gain. The *intention* behind this is very different, as it comes from manipulation, so even though they can appear similar in how they are put into action, it's the intention behind the action that gives those words a very different connotation. This puts it more in the realm of bribery than reinforcement.

With positive reinforcement, the person who is intended to benefit from the situation is the person on the receiving end, e.g., the child being able to have ice cream after cleaning their room. However, with bribery, it's the person placing the bribe who is intended to benefit, not the person on the receiving end.

I believe that this is a huge differentiation because a lot of people see situations as they are presented, but they don't necessarily see the bigger picture or the fuller meaning behind those situations.

Another context wherein I see this is prevalent and where this manifests, especially where intention is a differentiating factor, is the difference between a choice and a mistake.

When it comes to excuse vs. explanation, a lot of times, when people explain their behavior, they then also feel like this excuses the behavior. But I disagree and have pointed out that these are two different things. You can explain a behavior, but that doesn't automatically excuse this behavior.

Every word we use carries weight,
and how we label our behavior
shapes our accountability.

One of the things I also want to talk about is how this point is also important and relevant when identifying if someone is making a choice or a mistake.

A mistake is something that you did not intend to do. If I try to solve a math problem and make a mistake, then my answer is wrong. I didn't intend for that to happen. Maybe I miscalculated something, but it wasn't my intention to make this error.

Another example is a spelling error. I may think that a word is spelled a certain way, so that's how I spell it, but I was wrong, then I made a mistake.

Quite often, when we engage in behaviors that end up having negative consequences, especially when those negative consequences include punishment, we often refer to our behaviors as mistakes. However, it wasn't. It was a choice.

When I ran my groups in the prison, the inmates would often talk about their crimes and refer to them as mistakes. They would share with the group about when they made their mistake, and I would often redirect them and challenge them to reframe this language. I told them that they didn't make a mistake; they made a choice. By emphasizing that their behavior was a choice, it also emphasized their intention to engage in that behavior.

Their choices ultimately led to negative consequences, and it was only once they were experiencing those consequences that they could see that their behavior was a mistake, but ultimately, their behavior was a choice.

I think this is a very important distinction to make because it involves the element of accountability. If I make a mistake, that means that my intention was not to make a mistake. I intended to do right, so when I make a mistake, it's an honest mistake. It's an oversight. It's something that I was not aware of.

However, when you choose to do something negative, then that's not an oversight. When you hurt somebody to hurt them, that wasn't a mistake. That was a choice.

Even in my counseling practice, I use this as well because I think it's important to give clients accountability. Once you have accountability, then you have more control over how to change your actions.

If you make a mistake that was completely out of your control, then there wasn't anything you could do to change that. This also means that you have little control over changing this in the future because you didn't have any control over the situation. However, if you take accountability for the situation and you reframe your actions from a mistake to a choice, now you're empowering yourself and you're giving yourself more control to change your behavior in the future.

> If you had no control over it, you can't fix it.
> But if it was a choice,
> you can choose differently next time.

If you're looking at your life and certain things you look back at and determine, well, that was a mistake, it almost implies that there was an aspect about that mistake that was out of your control. But this also takes away your power over it.

However, if you can reframe this and identify that your past regret was not a mistake but was a choice that you made at the time, then you can acknowledge that if this is what you chose to do at that time, it led to negative consequences. Then, what are some things you can do differently to prevent those consequences? Now you have more control to change your outcome in the future.

Therefore, it's important to distinguish whether your actions were a choice or a mistake. A choice has an intention behind it. When you choose to do something wrong, that's not a mistake. You chose to do that, and there was an intention there. It also comes with accountability, which makes it easier for you to make those changes in the future and do better because you've held yourself accountable.

23
MAKING GOALS FEASIBLE

This chapter is about how to set realistic goals and how to best break big goals into smaller, more manageable goals. This is another type of subject that may seem simple and basic. However, it's another conversation that I have frequently with my clients because a lot of times, clients have an idea about what they want to work toward, but they don't always know how to go about accomplishing those goals.

Another factor is that sometimes clients look too far ahead, and they can only see the end goal, but they are unsure about how to make these steps manageable and realistic.

One way to break down goals into more realistic goals is to follow the SMART steps. SMART is an acronym that you may already be familiar with, and it's an easy-to-use system when addressing goals.

The S stands for specific, so defining your goals in a specific way and being specific about what it is you want to accomplish. Instead of defining your goal as "I want to be happy," ask yourself what that looks like for you specifically. It might be a recognition of smiling more than frowning, or getting to a place where it feels good to socialize with friends instead of isolating.

M stands for measurable, which is something you can see. Adding measurable to a goal to be happier means that you'll know that you're happier when you can see concrete signs of this, e.g., "I know that I'll feel better when I wake up in the morning and open the blinds to let sunlight in rather than living in darkness all day."

If your goal is a financial goal and your initial goal is to save, the M would encourage you to identify an amount to save up for.

The A stands for attainable. Is the goal you set for yourself something that can be reached? Is it something that you can work toward? This is when you may need to break your goals down into more manageable steps, as your long-term goal may be overwhelming, but the steps become attainable.

The R stands for realistic. Some goals are not realistic, and even though we're often taught that we can do anything we put our minds to, sometimes this is not the case. For example, if I set a goal to become the president of the United States, well, this is not a realistic goal for me because I was not born in the United States! I could set this goal, and it could be attainable theoretically as far as my abilities go, but still, it's not realistic for me.

Being realistic with your goals is very important because it also requires you to be honest about your expectations.

The T stands for time. This allows you to put a timeline on your goal, which helps you work toward your goal instead of putting it off indefinitely in the future. You may want to save up and then always spend your money and continue in a cycle of always wanting to save in the future. Putting a timeline on your goal helps you focus, especially if those goals are broken down into smaller steps, and each smaller step comes with its timeline.

The key to goal-setting isn't ambition, it's sustainability.

One of the conversations I often have with my clients in the realm of goal-setting is to find a starting place. Goals can be in any realm. You may have goals in the mental health realm that include working through anxiety, learning how to communicate better, learning how to manage symptoms, resolving trauma, to improving relationships in your life, etc.

Finding a realistic starting place for your goals is crucial because, in many ways, we struggle with that first step. This is the step that will eventually get you to your end goal. When you can identify that very first step, then you can build on from there.

For example, if I have a fitness goal of running a half-marathon but I've never run in my entire life, and it takes everything out of me to walk fast, then this may initially seem like an unrealistic goal. I'm not going to be able to get up and run 13.1 miles like that.

With this seemingly ambitious goal, I need to identify a first step. And maybe this first step is to be able to walk for one mile. A good average walking pace is about twenty minutes per mile, which I determine is very feasible, so maybe I will revise my starting goal to be able to walk two miles, i.e., walk for about forty minutes.

Once I've reached this goal, I can build from there. I can identify my steps toward my end goal before I even start them, but it's also important to remain flexible and be able to revise the steps as needed to continue keeping them realistic.

For example, I play the harp, and I also play the harp in a symphony. I started learning the harp as an adult, and I am by no means on a professional playing level. Every time I get new symphony music, it's often quite challenging, and I need to study hard to be able to play my pieces.

One of the ways I've learned how to study the pieces is that if I start to play some of those challenging pieces, it's too difficult, it's too complicated, and my brain and fingers don't work that fast together! So, I needed to find a system for myself that makes playing these challenging pieces manageable.

One of the systems I have is that my first goal is to simply learn the notes of the piece. I get familiar with the notes on the page, and whatever is written, that's what I play, no matter how long it takes me. I don't focus on the rhythm or the speed, only the notes.

When I can play the actual notes and get these in my fingers, then I play the notes according to the right rhythm on the page, but not at the tempo I'm supposed to be playing at. I find a tempo that is manageable for me but still allows me to keep the same rhythm as what is on the page. Sometimes, this tempo has been less than half of the speed of what I'm supposed to be playing, and I still stumble!

At this point, it may seem incredibly unrealistic to consider my end goal of having to play this piece more than twice the speed of what I'm playing now, but I only focus on the step that I'm on at that time, not the end goal.

I use an app on my phone where I can load a song and slow the tempo down, but it keeps the same intonation, so I can play along with a recording but at a slower pace. Sometimes, I play along with the recording at less than 50% of the original speed, but once I can master this speed consistently, then I start bumping up my speed from there.

Simply by focusing on this sequence of steps and focusing on one step at a time, I will reach my end goal, a goal that seemed impossible and incredibly intimidating when I first started it.

The helpful thing is to break down goals into what is more manageable. When I first play a piece, sometimes it's not manageable at all, but what is manageable is to identify how to play the first notes on the page. Play the first chord. Then, the second one. Then, play the third chord and then the fourth. If I stumble on the fourth chord, I stop to practice that fourth chord, and once I know it, I play the first through fourth chord and move on to the fifth, and so on.

This can be time-consuming and can feel tedious, but it gets me to where I need to be.

Another important thing to highlight about goal-setting and breaking down your goals into manageable steps is that you have to be realistic with your timelines.

A pattern I identify a lot is that when people set goals, they want to turn everything around. A conversation I had recently with a client was about helping them work through anger toward other people, anger at the political situation, anger about other people's driving, and anger in so many directions.

We had a conversation about how to reframe her thoughts and how to work toward more compassion, kindness, and patience toward others, especially while driving.

All the different conversations that came up in that particular session were about increasing kindness, being more compassionate, meditating every day, practicing breathing skills, not making assumptions about situations, and coming up with more positive assumptions about why people are doing what they're doing, and we ended up identifying a whole list of different things she could work on.

However, one thing I've seen over and over is that when people have a lot of things to work on, it becomes overwhelming to focus on all of those things simultaneously, and in the end, nothing gets done.

I relayed this back to her, and we brainstormed together so that she could focus on one thing. I asked her to identify out of the entire list of all these different things, what is one thing that she felt she might be able to do?

Out of the entire list, she said that when she is driving, she would like to wish impatient and aggressive drivers compassion and safety. She said that she would like to send them a positive thought and wish that they get to their destination safely.

We do this in our personal lives also, where we identify all these ideals that we need to include. We need to drink eight glasses of water every day. We need to meditate every day. We need to practice breathing skills every day, brush our teeth twice a day and floss, make a healthy breakfast every morning, make our beds, exercise, and do yoga; we need to pay attention to this and pay attention to that.

We get bombarded by so much information on how to have the perfect day, and so many different things that we should be doing daily, but I can tell you right now that if someone is not in the habit of any of those things, or even a fraction of these, then turning all of these things around all at once is not realistic.

The best place to start? Start by picking one. Maybe start with making your bed every morning. And when you're in the habit of making your bed every morning, pick a new thing.

This is an approach that is so much more effective because when you try to do all the things at once, you may be able to do this for a few days, but you won't sustain this, and you crash and burn.

Then you try again, finding a new start date to turn everything around, and you do this for a few days or weeks, but then you crash and burn again. So you try again but crash and burn again.

A year later, you're still at the same starting place of wanting to change so many things in your life, but not being consistent in your follow-through because you're taking on too much all at once. You're at the same starting place with your goals.

A better and more sustainable approach is to identify one thing you can focus on. You may identify that the one thing you're going to focus on is to start your day by making your bed every morning. So now you make your bed every morning, and two weeks later, you realize that it takes one to two minutes to make your bed, so now this habit has become easy and manageable.

Now, you identify another thing that you can focus on. You may identify that before you get out of your car before you go into the office, you choose to sit in your car for five minutes and practice some mindful breathing skills. Or you may choose to go into the office five minutes early, close your door, and do some breathing skills before you start your workday.

Once this has become manageable and you practice this consistently for a few weeks, you're in the habit of starting your day in a calmer state of mind, maybe even setting an intention for yourself at the start of every day that today you choose to go into work with a positive mindset.

Now you feel there's room to focus on another change, and so you set your new intention to focus on flossing your teeth every day instead of thinking about it, which is rarely.

So now, you focus on flossing your teeth every night, and this is the only new change you are making to your routine. Every day, you add this to your evening routine, and in a short period, you realize this takes a few minutes to do. It takes only a few weeks for you to get in the habit of flossing your teeth.

Over time, what happens is that when you change your approach to focus on only one thing at a time, it might seem like you're not making much progress because you're only focusing on one thing at a time instead of everything. You may believe that, ultimately, it's going to take you much longer to get to your end goal of turning all your negative habits into positive ones. However, instead of being in the cycle of crashing and burning and setting a new start date, you're creating habits that last.

If you start by simply focusing on one change at a time, and then a year later, you see where you're at compared to your starting place, you'd be extremely surprised at your results because you're taking steps toward your goals that are manageable.

What often happens in session is that we try to focus on one goal, one manageable change. For example, take someone who has depression. They have low motivation, they experience low energy and low mood, and any kind of household chore is way too overwhelming because when they think about cleaning up their place, it involves laundry and cooking and cleaning, and tidying up, etc.

None of those things sound appealing, and nothing gets done. If this is the case, then I have a conversation with my clients about identifying out of all the things that need to get done, what is one thing they feel is manageable for them, no matter how small.

I ask them to identify what the one thing is that they feel they could do every day, even if that's the only thing they get done that day. Maybe they will say that they can pick their clothes up off the floor and put them in the laundry basket. So, this one thing becomes the focus.

It could be to get up and start the day by taking a shower. Even if that's the only thing they accomplish that day, they have done the one thing they set out to do. Even if they go back to bed after taking that shower, that's okay because they accomplished the one thing they set for themselves for the day.

The nice thing about setting an earlier-in-the-day goal and accomplishing this goal, like making the bed or taking a shower, is that, quite often, it kick starts a motivation that allows them to accomplish more things throughout their day.

I did have a client who had a diagnosis of depression, and one of the things she noticed was that when she was experiencing symptoms of depression, all her regular daily chores became too overwhelming for her to the point that nothing got done.

What she did was set one goal for herself, and this goal was to make her bed in the morning. The reason she chose this particular goal was that she knew that if she made her bed in the morning, her bed would be clean and tidy, which would prompt her to tidy up her room, which would then prompt her to get ready for the day and get dressed and put her clothes away.

She recognized that the one act of making her bed set this whole ball into motion, and this is how she was able to get her day going.

The big question with goal-setting is to identify how you start at a place that is reasonable for you. Maybe you want to save $10,000, but you have debts. You notice that every time you try to put money aside into a savings account, and then you get your bills, you always end up using your money from your savings account to pay your bills, and you get nowhere. This becomes an unattainable goal.

What would be a better starting place? It could be about shifting your focus from saving to reducing your debts. It may be about creating a budget and identifying what you need to do to reduce debt and pay off everything first. This would be the first step.

The reasonable starting place that you then identify is reducing debt rather than putting money into savings. And even though you haven't saved anything, you're working toward this end goal. By putting money into savings, you may believe you're working toward your goal of $10,000, but if every month you use that money to pay bills, then you're not.

By revising your goal to make it more realistic, you're saving yourself from the cycle of putting money into savings and then using it for bills, putting money back into savings, and using it again for debt. You're going to get closer to your goal of $10,000 when you focus on reducing your debt first, because then whatever you will be able to put in savings after reducing debt will be able to stay in savings.

You have to find a realistic starting place. It has to be small, and it has to be manageable. It can even be something that sounds incredibly silly, but if that's your starting place, then that's where you start.

There are so many different types of goals that people have. It could be career goals, or you want to go back to college, but you have no idea what for. The first step may be to take a questionnaire to identify your strengths. Or you may work on connecting with someone like a career adviser who can help you identify your strengths in a career field.

The main points regarding goal-setting are how you identify what you want to work on, how you break it down in a way that makes it realistic for you, and how you find your starting place. How do you identify that first step?

When you identify that you want to save $10,000, what's the first step? Do you have to create a budget? Maybe a few things need to be in place before you're even in a position to put money into savings, so identifying these initial steps becomes very important to make your goal realistic.

If you work on setting up a budget, you may find that your

expenses are higher than your income. If that's the case, then you'll never be able to save, as this will become unrealistic and unattainable. Your goals would have to be revised to focus on either reducing expenses, increasing income, or both.

There are usually several different ways that we can achieve our goals, but the key is in that first step. It's about staying focused on the current step. If you only focus on the next step in front of you instead of the whole thing, if that's all you do, inevitably, you will get to where you're going.

An analogy I often use with clients when I talk about the importance of staying focused on the current step is to imagine that I'm in California. Then I decide that I want to walk to the East Coast. Everyone around me will think I'm crazy and that this goal is ridiculous and impossible. That's a distance of 3000 miles, and how could I be so absurd?

However, if all I do is put one foot in front of another and start walking, and this is all I focus on, no matter how long it may take me, the inevitable result is that I will, at some point, reach the East Coast.

The reason is that's where I'm heading, and as long as I'm not standing still or moving west, I can only get closer and closer to my goal until I get there. Inevitably. Even if I take baby steps, it's still inevitable.

And this applies to any kind of goal. Say you want to work on weight loss, or you have a fitness goal. Once you find your starting place and you begin working toward your goal, as long as you're moving in the direction of where you want to go, no matter how slowly, then every step is one step toward your goal, and you will inevitably get there.

It applies to the goal of running a half-marathon. If you've never run before, then find your starting place. Maybe that's walking one or two miles. When you can walk two miles, you either focus on covering that distance a little faster, to a jog, or increasing your distance, but either way, you are moving in the direction of your goal, which is the important thing.

As long as you are continuously working *toward* the direction of your goal, you will get there, no matter what.

> Consistency beats intensity.
> It's not about how fast,
> it's about how long you can keep going.

One of the biggest things that puts people off from staying on track with their goals is seeing the big picture, because this can quite often feel too overwhelming. Running a half-marathon when you're struggling with walking two miles is very daunting and discouraging. Saving $10,000 when you're in debt can be overwhelming. Losing fifty pounds may seem impossible.

If you find yourself in this position, begin by identifying your end goal. Once you've identified your outcome, then break this down into smaller, more manageable goals. When you have identified these steps, find your starting place; a starting place that is manageable, sustainable, and that is something that you can follow through with. And once you're there, simply focus on the step that's in front of you and keep moving forward from there.

24
STOP COMPARING

This next chapter is about why it's important to stop comparing yourself to other people. Of course, you already know that you shouldn't do this, so I'm not telling you anything new.

You already know that you shouldn't compare yourself to others because everyone is on their journey, but it's very important and meaningful to consider this statement and to truly grasp that every single journey is vastly unique.

I see all too often that people feel inadequate about themselves when they compare themselves to others. If you already feel inadequate or flawed in some way, then it doesn't matter what is going on with the other person or what is happening. You'll find something to confirm this already existing belief about yourself.

If you already struggle with low self-worth and you don't believe you're deserving of positive things or that other people must have a much better life than you, then you're going to see this in others. If you believe this, then it doesn't matter how positive things are going in your life, you're still going to find confirmation of the perfection of other people's lives in what you see.

There are a few things I want to talk about within this realm. The first thing is, as a mental health counselor, I'm privy to people's lives behind the scenes. There are so many times that people present very well, and they present as if they have the perfect relationship or the perfect career, or they are nice and kind to others. They can seem like the kind of people we strive to be.

But when they come into my office and talk about all the different things they are worrying about or about their struggles, their lives are no different from yours or mine. You may be surprised at how many people struggle with exactly the things you think are going perfectly for them.

> You only ever see a glimpse of someone else's story,
> never the whole script.

You may see a person who is very social and outgoing. They have a lot of friends, and they succeed at everything they do. This very individual may be in my office with incredibly high levels of anxiety, barely able to function because all their energy and focus have gone into presenting a good image to others, leaving them depleted in other areas of their life.

This same person may be deeply unhappy, but they're putting on a very brave face to everyone else when, deep down, they feel empty and lonely, but you would never see this side of them.

You may also think that the couple you always see is the perfect couple. They never argue, and they always seem so supportive of each other, and they seem so connected and committed to each other. However, this same couple may be sitting in my office with some significant relational issues, causing them to be on the verge of divorce. And this is a side of them that you don't see.

We make a lot of assumptions about everything, and I believe that this is human nature. It's how we make sense of the world, and it's how we put things together.

However, we also make a lot of assumptions about others, but we always only ever see a glimpse of what is going on in their world. We can be very quick to make assumptions about somebody's life, but ultimately, we don't know.

It becomes important for us to refocus our attention back on our lives and use our experience as a starting ground because, in the end, it's only this that we know to be fact.

A healthier reframe could be to see different people and the things you believe are so perfect in others as role models rather than a fact and a reason to feel worse about yourself.

The emphasis is no longer about seeing how great someone else is, which highlights your lacking, but that another person's strengths become an inspiration for you to strive to get to this place in your own life. In this way, you're not putting yourself down in any way, but instead, you're using that perspective as a strength because you're now using it as an inspiration and role-model rather than a comparison.

**Someone else's success doesn't mean your failure.
There's room for both.**

Another reason why you need to stop comparing is that, often, you will only ever see a result. More often than not, you don't see all the hard work that goes into something. You often don't see the hard work, the strife, and the struggles people go through to get to where they are now. When you admire someone, you're only looking at the result.

For example, say there's a guitar player you admire, and this person plays the guitar like nobody's business. You may get discouraged because you think you'll never be able to play the guitar as well as they do. They're so good at playing the guitar, and now it feels daunting and discouraging. Every time you hear how amazing this guitar player plays, you feel inadequate and incompetent.

Every time you listen to this player, you're reminded of how good you're not. But what you've also never seen is that particular guitar player going through the same struggles as you are going through today.

You never see that guitar player in their first week of playing, struggling to play Row Your Boat. You don't see them getting impatient with themselves for getting something wrong over and over again. They have also gone through a learning curve to be able to get to their playing level today.

The same applies when you see athletes. You see your favorite athletes winning their competitions, but there's a lot of hard work and frustration and competitions lost, which is part of their history, too.

You don't see the hard days and the struggles. What you see is the result. So what you're doing is comparing your state now to someone who has already accomplished your end goal.

This is not fair! It's not fair because the person you are comparing yourself to now was once where you are now, but you're expecting yourself to already be as good. It's not fair because you've deprived yourself of seeing the hard work they've put in, and you're not considering this in your journey.

It's important to remind yourself to identify the story you're telling yourself. You have to pay attention to the language you use about yourself about a situation. If you see someone and they have traits that you desire, what are you telling yourself about it? Is your language toward yourself positive or negative? Can you recognize that someone looks beautiful but then automatically believe you'll never be able to look this beautiful too? Does your comparison now reflect negatively on your own life and highlight your negative self-talk?

Or does your perspective of someone, such as their flawless skin, encourage you to work toward those same goals yourself? Instead of instantly feeling bad about your skin, maybe you could even ask what skin routine they use, which encourages you to feel better about your skin.

The difference between those two responses is the story you're telling yourself. In one version, you're recognizing that someone has something better, which emphasizes a lack. In the other version, you're recognizing that someone has something better, and you are happy for them, and it can even teach you how to have more of this in your own life.

One of the beautiful things about life is that there's room for everyone to feel positive. When someone experiences happiness in their life, it doesn't mean that there's no room for you to have happiness, also, but there's plenty of room for both of you to be happy.

The same goes for success. Because someone else is successful doesn't mean that there's no room for you to be successful. Or rich. Or connected to someone. Multiple people can experience those things at the same time.

The whole phenomenon of comparing can get very toxic because it tends to highlight something that you feel is missing in your life, however, there is no lack because someone has what you want. As I mentioned before, when I see clients in my practice, they could be struggling in the areas that others think are so perfect.

One point I want to highlight when you compare yourself to others, especially if this results in highlighting a lack in yourself, is that you then engage in all-or-nothing thinking, which is a thinking error. This is probably one of the most common types of thinking errors, and we do this often.

Some versions of all-or-nothing thinking could be, "If you're not my friend, then you're my enemy," "You either love me or hate me," or "If I don't pass this test, then I'm a failure." These are thinking errors because the presence or absence of one does not imply the presence or absence of another, yet in our minds, it does.

I may not necessarily be your friend, but that doesn't mean I'm your enemy, either. I may not particularly love you, but that doesn't mean I hate you either. I can fail a test and still be successful.

Yet when we compare ourselves to others in this way, it's all-or-nothing. In your mind, there's only room for one, but this type of thinking needs to be challenged. If one of your friends announces that they got a significant promotion and will be making a significant amount of money, you may suddenly feel inadequate and a failure because you're not making the same amount of money.

However, there's room for both of you to be successful. Your friend can be mega-rich and super-successful, and you can also be successful and comfortable even without being mega-rich.

Another point I want to highlight when it comes to comparing yourself to others is that if you're going to compare yourself to someone else in this moment, then you also have to take on and consider their entire history.

Take, for example, someone who has had a lot of challenges in their life, e.g., maybe they've come from a history of abuse and neglect. Now, they're working on navigating healthy relationships, and they see their peers in healthy relationships. They see that it seems to come so easily and naturally to their peers to be in healthy relationships, and now, they become very discouraged at having to do so much work to be in a healthy relationship themselves.

Seeing how easy it is for their peers to be in healthy relationships can emphasize how difficult it is for them to have the same thing, and they may feel inadequate at building healthy relationships because they feel they should be able to do this like their peers.

However, if this person is going to compare themselves to their peers, then they also have to compare their peers' entire past. Would their peer, who is very good at creating social connections and meaningful relationships, still have those same meaningful relationships if they had the same upbringing as them?

I see this happen a lot, for example, with clients who end up going back to school after a long period, and they are a lot older than their peers. Quite often, they may compare themselves to their younger peers. They may vocalize their wish that they had the same opportunity, but here they are, in college at an older age, and it's so much more of a struggle to learn because they haven't been to school in so long, whereas their peers are fresh out of high school, and so their learning is fresh!

They are comparing their situation in the present to their peers. If this person truly wants to compare their situation to their younger peers, then they also have to add their background to their peers.

Would those peers still be as adaptable to learning had they also taken a break from learning for the same number of years? Would they navigate this technology as easily if they had also not been on computers for as long? Would it be as easy for them to study if they also hadn't read a textbook for many years?

When we compare ourselves to others, we also have to consider their background. Yes, we cannot compare ourselves to others because everyone is on their journey, but everyone also *comes from* a different journey. And this is the part that is often not emphasized.

Everyone also has their past, and that greatly influences how easy things are for them today. For example, people who are in unhealthy relationships over and over likely have not received healthy role-modeling or have not witnessed what healthy relationships look like. Relationships then become a whole learning curve for them as opposed to someone whose parents have had a solid relationship, and they've witnessed healthy role-modeling that models nurturing and respect.

The same applies to compassion. If someone grows up in an angry household where everyone thinks about themselves, then compassion may be harder to access.

Like the musician who picks up a guitar and can play, maybe they have a greater musical ability because they've played other musical instruments in the past and already know how to read music, whereas a beginner to anything musical is going to struggle more because they have more to learn.

Yes, everyone is on their journey, but what I think is more important is that everyone has their history. Everyone has their challenges, and this is the factor that determines where people are in life.

It might even be worth reframing comparisons, and if something comes so easily to someone else, instead of this reflecting all the things you're not, I wonder what it would be like for you to reframe that into being happy for that person.

Do your best to refrain from making assumptions about others when you tend to compare. Consider your journey and your history and focus on that. If you do want to make a comparison, then instead of comparing yourself to others, I challenge you to compare yourself to an earlier version of yourself. Maybe then it becomes easier to recognize your growth, progress, and success.

25
CHANGING EXPECTATIONS

In this chapter, I'd like to talk about creating realistic expectations. Some of the conversations I've had with different clients are when they've felt dissatisfied with something. This could be a relationship or some other aspect of their life.

What I see is that they have certain expectations of other people or life, but ultimately, they become disappointed because those expectations were not met.

One of the misconceptions is that when they change their expectations, they sometimes feel like this is the same as lowering their expectations, and this doesn't feel right. When you lower your expectations, you're not striving for the best for yourself. By lowering your expectations, you stop striving for all that you want.

However, when you change your expectations, it doesn't mean that you're necessarily lowering your expectations. What you're doing is not setting yourself up for disappointment. You allow yourself to be more flexible in what to expect, but you're also being more flexible in your circumstances. You start to recognize and understand the reality of the situation and, therefore, what is realistic.

Say, for example, you're a teacher, and you have a student who is an A student. Passing tests comes naturally to them, and academically, they do very well. Then you have another student who is struggling so much. This student spends so much time on homework. They constantly struggle with understanding the material, and it's all they can do to get Cs.

When the C student studies hard on something and suddenly gets an A on a test, then this A is naturally celebrated! The teacher gives their praises and makes a big deal out of it.

Now, the A student thinks to themselves that this isn't fair. They're always pulling in A's, so why should the other students get all this attention and praise when this is what they do all the time?

The reason is that it isn't about the A. It's about recognizing where someone is and meeting them where they're at. It's about recognizing that the A for the C student is a much bigger deal than the A is for the A student. Their baselines are very different. It becomes relative.

Changing your expectations doesn't mean you've stopped caring, it means you've started adapting.

It can feel frustrating and unfair when you're always doing what you need to do, and then someone else does exactly what you do and gets celebrated for it. However, it's all relative. Maybe that individual hasn't always been able to do what comes so naturally to you, and therefore, this thing becomes a big deal to this other individual.

This outlook becomes important when it comes to changing your expectations and meeting people where they're at. This is not the same as lowering your expectations because several positive things come out of meeting someone where they're at and changing your expectations accordingly.

First, you're avoiding the negative feelings that come with not having your expectations met repeatedly. Maybe, for a certain individual, you're setting your expectations too high.

Second, a lot of times, what happens is that because you're taking away those higher restrictions, that person now has a little more room to grow. You might even see progress faster because now they are being encouraged with where they're at, not with where you want them to be right now.

For example, say you're in a relationship, and your partner doesn't communicate very well. They've never learned how to communicate well or express their feelings, and maybe they grew up in a family where any discussion about emotions was avoided. Maybe you come from a family that has been nurturing and affectionate, and feelings were validated.

To expect your partner to be as open emotionally and as nurturing and affectionate might not be a realistic expectation because they're not there yet.

Then, when you want to have these deep and elaborate conversations with them and share your feelings, and you want them to share their feelings, you're probably setting yourself up for repeated disappointment because this is not realistic for your partner.

When you can recognize this, then you can maybe decide to take baby steps with your partner. Maybe you decide to have smaller conversations about things. When you do this, you may feel like you're lowering your expectations because you're not having these deeper, elaborate, emotion-based conversations. However, what you're doing is changing your expectations to meet them where they're at, and this is what allows them to grow.

Those negative emotions that you feel afterward, or the pressure they may be feeling to share out of their comfort zone, are now removed, and now they have the flexibility to grow. This will allow them to feel better about learning and growing, and it will result in a more positive outcome for you.

This is one of the themes that comes back in counseling. When you set expectations for yourself, whether those expectations are from other people or goals that you set for yourself, are you being realistic with your expectations?

Maybe your expectations need to change. When you're constantly striving for the best, then if you're not doing your best, it's not good enough. Now you add pressure. You're more likely to fail if you set your expectations too high and only accept perfection.

But if you can recognize your starting place, your baseline, and you focus on growing from there, there's more flexibility and freedom and a lot less pressure to grow. This is how you can set yourself up for greater progress.

Your progress should be measured from your starting point, not someone else's.

I even see this manifest when people have their own goals. Say you have a goal in the realm of self-growth, like working on managing anxiety, and you identify your end goal as never being anxious. Then anything other than never being anxious is now not good enough.

This goal wouldn't even be realistic. If you're making significant progress but you're still experiencing anxiety, in your mind, you haven't met your goal because you haven't resolved your anxiety.

A more realistic way to address this is to first recognize your baseline. Where are you at right now? And from there, what does progress look like? How would you recognize progress?

For example, take someone who experiences panic attacks every day. For this individual to resolve their panic attacks from every day to never may be too ambitious for an initial goal. Then, when we start to work together on how to manage anxiety and panic attacks, and this individual begins to learn healthy coping skills, over time, they may come into my office and tell me they are still experiencing panic attacks.

From their perspective, they're not making any progress because yesterday, they still had a panic attack. However, if we look closer at their recent history, maybe they also acknowledge that when they had their panic attack yesterday, they were able to recognize the symptoms as it was happening and work through them faster. Or maybe the panic attack they had yesterday wasn't as severe as usual. Maybe they even recognize that this panic attack was the first panic attack they had had in two weeks.

When we then refer to their treatment plan, which stated that they were having panic attacks every day, and now they see that this was their first panic attack in two weeks, then that is very significant progress. They are working on resolving anxiety, and they are working on their treatment goals.

The reframe is about how you can change your expectations to make them more realistic and to make them in a way that there's room for progress and growth.

Many times, when the goals and expectations are too restrictive, there is no room to grow. There has to be flexibility.

Another aspect of changing your expectations is that it's not the same as not caring. For example, if you don't keep the end goal in sight but only focus on the first step instead of the last step, then you may think that the last step isn't important anymore. It also may look the same as not caring, but this isn't the case. You still care about the end goal, but you refocus your attention on what is more realistic and what is more likely to change now, which is going to allow you to reach your end goal more effectively.

I've had these very conversations with clients before. Some clients have even said that if they don't have these expectations of someone else, then maybe they should stop caring, and then it won't be a big deal anymore.

Don't stop caring. Instead, allow your end goals to exist, but meet someone where they're at. Take the example of being in a relationship with someone who doesn't communicate well. Now there's a communication breakdown, and even though you want to have deep and meaningful conversations with someone, it never happens.

It might be easy to tell yourself that if you stopped caring about it, then it wouldn't be a big deal. You may think that if you have to change your expectations, then you have to lower your expectations, which means you should stop caring about them.

The problem with this is that when you stop caring and you lower your expectations in this way, you've also stopped working toward your goal. This is a big difference.

Instead of not caring and lowering your expectations, which results in you never reaching your end goal, you're changing your expectations to make your expectations more realistic and to allow room for growth and learning. When they've reached this step, you can move on to the next step, etc.

This way, you're continuing to work toward your end goal, and this is the more productive way.

Changing your expectations in a situation is not the same as lowering your expectations because changing your expectations is about identifying a more realistic path to get to your end goal. Lowering your expectations doesn't allow for this.

Changing your expectations is also not the same as not caring for the same reason. When you change your expectations, you continue to work on the end goal. You're making these more manageable and fairer. When you stop caring then you stop making progress, and this is where you stay stagnant.

Say, for example, you want to get yourself out of debt. You want to be financially independent, but you have debts to pay. You need roommates to help pay the bills. Your goal is to have your place, but in that moment, it might feel incredibly overwhelming.

When you continue in that pattern, you may feel disappointed in yourself because you still have not achieved your goal. However, when you change your expectations then you can look at your situation and ask yourself what a more realistic goal could be.

Maybe you identify that for you to be financially independent, and if you want to own your place with no roommates, and if you want to be debt-free, out of all those expectations, the first thing you need to do is to address the debt.

You haven't lowered your expectations by changing your goal from owning your place to getting out of debt. That end goal is still there. You're changing your expectations in the present because you recognize what is more realistic and what you can work toward in the present.

I know this theme has been presented in previous chapters because it's very important in many ways. I'm talking about the same kind of theme, but from a different angle.

In the example above, the first step you may identify is that you need to start getting yourself out of debt. This is an expectation that you can start working toward.

So now you create a budget plan, and you figure out how much you need to make every month to start bringing your debts down. You could even break this down further into monthly goals and identify how much you want to pay off every month.

Then, you keep moving forward from there. In no way have you ever lowered your expectations at all because, ultimately, you're still working toward that end goal of owning your place. You haven't stopped caring either, because the entire reason why you're creating these smaller goals is precisely that. After all, you care, and you want to work toward your goal.

You've now changed your expectations, and now you're meeting yourself where you're at, in your current situation. You identify what you can work on in that moment, and this becomes way more productive.

In that moment, it may not be feasible to have a place of your own without roommates, so that's not a realistic expectation because if this were your current expectation of yourself, you wouldn't be meeting yourself where you're at.

These are the important distinctions between lowering your expectations, not caring, and changing your expectations.

You have to identify your starting place, and it's important to be realistic when identifying this. You may not like this starting place, but it's important to be honest in recognizing where you're at, or where other people are at. Only from that point can you start moving forward.

I've used this example in a previous chapter also, but say, for example, you're a personal trainer and two people come to you with the same goal of running a half-marathon. One of those two people runs regularly, and the other person has never run before. You wouldn't give them the same training plan. Instead, you would identify where they're at and adjust your training plan accordingly. For the beginner runner, you may get them to run one to two miles first, whereas with the experienced runner, you may start with six miles.

You're not lowering your expectations of the beginner runner because you still have confidence that they will reach the same end goal as the experienced runner. You're simply changing your expectations in-the-moment to make that end goal more attainable.

If you give the beginner runner the same expectations as the experienced runner, and you expect them to be able to run a 5k by next week, then when they're not able to do this, you're going to be disappointed in them. They feel disappointed in themselves also because they weren't able to meet your expectations.

You would never start their training in this way! That would be unfair, but this is often what we do with ourselves and with others in many areas of our lives. We place these unrealistic expectations on people because we expect other people to be where *we* are, and this is not fair.

If you're emotionally very intelligent, you cannot expect everyone else to be emotionally very intelligent either. A lot of people simply aren't. The same goes for regular intelligence. If you're very smart and know a lot of things, you can't expect everyone else to know what you know.

If you're good at something, you cannot expect other people to be as good at that same thing.

We have to become a little bit more flexible with how we see situations and how we look at the world. We also have to apply this flexibility when we see others and with the expectations we place on others.

What happens when we do this is, first, we're saving ourselves from disappointments by not setting ourselves and others up for failure, and second, we're increasing flexibility and allowing more room for growth and progress.

26
ADAPTABILITY

In this chapter, I'd like to talk about the importance of adaptability and flexibility. A lot of people, over time, get caught up in rigid thinking, and this can create a lot of barriers because it gives people expectations of how things should or shouldn't be.

This, in turn, can create negative emotions because when you're in a situation, and you don't agree with the situation, and you believe that the situation should or shouldn't be a certain way, what that implies is feeling like something should be a certain way, it means that it isn't.

> The question isn't "Why is this happening?"
> but "What can I do with this?"

This creates a lot of negative emotions because what we're also doing is we're getting fixated on something that we cannot change.

This creates conflict, anger, and frustration because there are many times when we get caught up in a situation, and it doesn't feel fair, even rightly so.

There could be many aspects of the situation that are not okay, but the problem is, we can be angry or frustrated over a situation, but sometimes we get stuck there.

I think it's very important for us to have the skills to adapt and be flexible within our situation. I also think it's important for us to be able to recognize what we can do within our situation.

When I talk about the fact that we get stuck in situations that we cannot control, one of the biggest types of situations that are not in our control are the behaviors of other people.

What other people say or do, or how people respond to different situations, is out of our control. People are going to say what they're going to say, and people are going to do what they're going to do, and we have no control over this.

We can influence someone's response to us based on our approach to them, e.g., if we approach someone defensively or abruptly, then we can probably expect a more defensive response in return. However, if we approach someone in a kind and open manner, then we're influencing their response.

We cannot control what people think, say, or do. We can sometimes influence this, but as a rule, people are going to do and say what they want, and they're going to believe what they believe, and we have limited control over this.

However, we place expectations on people about what they should or shouldn't be doing, and this is when we create negative emotions for ourselves.

One example that I'm sure a lot of readers will relate to is road rage. You see other drivers on the road being aggressive or driving crazy. Everyone has their irritations when it comes to driving. And every time you experience an aggressive or "stupid" driver, you create negative emotions for yourself.

The problem is, whenever you find that you're frustrated or angry in a situation, what's happening is a version of *should* or *shouldn't*. Let me say that again. Anger is always a response to a version of should or shouldn't.

When someone is driving, and they cut you off, when you experience anger, it's because you're thinking that person *shouldn't* have cut you off. Or when you're driving and someone is tailgating you, and this is frustrating you, in a sense what you're thinking is they *shouldn't* be tailgating you.

Another example is if you hit every single red light and you're getting increasingly impatient because every single traffic light you approach turns red. What you're thinking is that the traffic light *should* be green when you approach it.

So now you're getting frustrated, but even worse, you're getting frustrated over a situation that is completely out of your control. The simple fact is that you're not going to change the traffic light patterns, and you're not going to change the way other people drive.

What you are doing is giving everyone else control over how you feel because what's happening is if everyone is a good driver and everyone gives you space, and if everyone drives the way you need them to, then you'll have a good day behind the wheel. Well, good luck with that!

In situations like this, we need to find a way to take control of our emotions because when you become frustrated over situations that are not in your control, especially when the source of your frustration is the behavior of other people, then they have control over your emotions. The way that we take control back is to be more flexible in our situation and identify how we can best adapt to our situation.

One of the reasons I love adaptability is because it is the number one characteristic of a species surviving extinction. When species survive over many centuries and eras, it's not strength or intelligence that causes their survival. It's the ability to adapt to their environment.

Adaptability comes with a few added characteristics. When a species adapts to its new environment, it doesn't mean it likes the new environment. It doesn't have to like the changes. It doesn't necessarily agree or approve of the changes, but the species recognizes that this is how it is.

When you can recognize the facts of your situation, that this is how it is, whether you like it or not, then you will have a greater ability to adapt to it.

You can adapt to a situation and at the same time not like it. But what you're doing when you do recognize and acknowledge the facts of a situation is that you're taking back control.

You're now giving yourself power by recognizing what you can do within your situation. We cannot control the circumstances that we're in, and many times, we can't control what happens to us. The only thing that we can ever do within a situation is manage how we respond to the things that happen to us.

We've all heard this before - it's not about what happens to us, it's about how we respond - but this is the only thing that we do have any control over.

One thing that I will say is that it's okay to be frustrated or upset at your situation, but it's important not to stay stuck there. I know I've talked about this before because your feelings are valid, but you also want to work through those emotions.

Being flexible and adaptable goes like this. Instead of experiencing road rage and being angry at every driver, take back your power. Don't let other people's decisions on the road affect you. Stop telling yourself what drivers should or shouldn't be doing. The way for you to get your power back and adapt to your frustrating situation is to acknowledge that, wow, there are a lot of distracted drivers on the road, and so many people seem to be in a hurry, so how can I now create a pleasant driving experience for myself *despite* all these factors being present?

Rage doesn't change the traffic light, but it will ruin your drive.

Even with all these factors in place, how can you continue to stay calm and content behind the wheel? That is how you change the way you feel. Only then. Because what you're doing is taking the shoulds and shouldn'ts out of the picture.

"That person shouldn't drive like that!" Well, maybe you're right, but it doesn't change the fact that the person *is* driving like that. As long as you keep telling yourself how that person should or shouldn't be driving, what this means is that you'll only feel better and calmer when that person changes how they drive. Now, this random person has full control over how you feel!

When you do this, you rely on things completely out of your control for how you feel, which is unproductive, very disempowering, and makes no sense at all. Yet we do this all the time!

The reframe is, how can I continue to have a pleasant driving experience *despite* these obnoxious drivers being on the road?

This is not the same as saying that you're okay with how other people drive. You're not being asked to like how other people drive. It also doesn't mean that you approve of your situation. What you're focusing on instead is asking yourself how you can continue to be in control of your emotions *despite* all of these factors being in place.

For example, you could work on showing more compassion toward other drivers so that when someone is in a hurry, instead of muttering swear words under your breath, you may instead wish them patience and that they get to where they need to be safely. When you take this kind of approach instead of an angry one, it's also so much easier to let go of the experience.

You can easily move on from this exchange because you're not keeping yourself stuck in these negative emotions.

Let me give you a more extreme example to highlight how adaptability to your environment allows you to have control over your emotions. Say you get into a bad car accident that has left you significantly limited in some way, e.g., you lose a leg. Of course, there's going to be a period of grief that you're going to go through. You're going to be angry at the world, you're going to be upset, sad, and go through a whole rollercoaster of emotions.

This rollercoaster of emotions would very much be justified as you're going through the grief process. However, if you keep yourself angry over time and you stay bitter about your situation, then in the end, you're keeping yourself stuck in an unpleasant state of mind. You can continue to stay angry at the world, which we now know includes some elements of should and shouldn't.

"This should never have happened!" You're absolutely right, and also it did. "I should still be able to walk like I used to!" Again, you're right, and also, you can't. "I should still have both legs!" Yes, you should, but also you don't.

You can be 100% correct in all these thoughts, but when you get stuck there, you continue to focus on the elements of the situation that are out of your control.

At one point, to get control back over your emotions, you have to identify the aspects of your situation that you have no control over. And in this situation, one of the aspects that you don't have control over is what happened in the past. You've lost your leg, and there's no going back from that. Another thing that is completely out of your control is that now you have one leg. This will also never change.

The adaptability piece is to identify what is within these parameters and limitations, and with all these factors in place and considering all the facts of the situation, what are some things you *can* do?

What are the things you *can* do even though you got into the accident and despite having one leg? Now you're adapting. Now you're being flexible to your situation, and now you're evolving to your new environment.

You evolve by adapting to your situation and by asking yourself what you can do despite the circumstances. This is how you survive your situation, again emphasizing that this doesn't mean that you like your situation, it doesn't mean that you agree with your situation, and it doesn't mean that you approve of it.

It also doesn't mean that you're giving in to your situation. What you're doing is empowering yourself because you're recognizing the things within your limited situation that you do have some control over.

With this new mindset in place, you can now focus on what you can do. You may now consider what you can add to your environment to make life easier with one leg. Maybe you focus on shifting things around in your house so that things become more accessible, or maybe you focus on pursuing medical advice for a prosthetic to allow for greater freedom and mobility. Or maybe you can access a support group for others who have lost a limb, so you don't feel so alone in your experience.

The mind shift that happens is now you start to move forward. You can live your whole life without liking it or agreeing with it, and at the same time, you're also allowing yourself to get your power and control back, especially over your emotions.

A lighter example could be that you're driving, and on the way, you get a flat tire. So now you must pull over on the side of the road, and you're angry because you need to be somewhere. With that anger comes the "should" and "shouldn't" thinking. "I shouldn't have gotten this flat tire!" True, but you did.

That initial anger and frustration are appropriate because now you've been inconvenienced, and you're probably going to be late. Your feelings are valid, and this is a normal response, but keeping yourself stuck there and continuing with negative thinking is not going to resolve your situation.

Being adaptable to your situation is about recognizing the facts of your situation, including the facts that are out of your control. Well, the fact is that you have a flat tire, and you're stuck on the side of the road. Now, what within those facts, those parameters, do you have an element of control?

Now, you ask yourself what you *can* do in this environment with these parameters in place. The fact is, whether you like it or not, you're on the side of the road. Whether you like it or not, you have a flat tire. Whether you like it or not, you're going to be late to where you were going.

Now, what can you do with all these facts in place? Now, you focus on problem-solving and recognize that the first thing you can do is call the place you were headed to explain your situation and inform them you'll likely be late. Then you can focus on maybe changing your tire or if you don't know how or have the tools, you can call someone to help you.

Because you're acknowledging the facts of your situation, now you can focus on solutions and results and only now are you going to be able to move through your situation. It doesn't mean that at any moment in time, you liked being in this situation. What you have done is adapted and evolved.

I talk a lot about adaptability with my clients because what I also see is that people get stuck in a line of thinking. And many times, I would argue all the time a version of what they're stuck in is something that is out of their control.

One very prevalent type of situation is the political situation. People have very opposite and outspoken ideas about so many things. This is not going to change. But it causes people to stay upset over situations completely out of their control. You are not going to change the mindset of millions of people; it's not going to happen. However, you can keep yourself stuck there.

You can be angry at the state of the world and yes, be frustrated and be upset, but don't keep yourself stuck there. I've seen so many people keeping themselves angry and keeping themselves in a very negative state of mind, and it's all over situations they have no control over. Therefore, the pattern, the trend, is that they're going to continue to feel angry for the rest of their lives.

All the tools that these angry individuals have to create more positive emotions for themselves are right there, within their reach, because it's the outlook and thinking patterns that are creating these negative emotions. But instead, they give control to everyone else and allow everyone else's behaviors to keep them stuck.

If you find yourself continuously upset, whether this is over a political situation or a social situation, then maybe the reframe is to focus on adapting to your situation.

Now you can ask yourself, what are the facts of your situation? It doesn't matter whether you like them or not; what are the facts? The fact is that this is the state of the world, this is the state of society, this is what people are saying and doing, and this is how things are at the moment.

When you keep yourself angry about the situation, you're essentially saying that you're going to feel better when all these things are no longer in place. Well, good luck with that!

The healthier and more productive approach is to ask yourself, despite the state of the world and awful things happening, how can you continue to create more pleasant emotions for yourself, even with all these things in place?

This is the key. When you ask yourself this question, you may change your focus to your immediate connections and the friendships that are right around you. Focusing on these will increase positive emotions. You may choose to focus on having fun experiences with friends and family because this is what can change the way you feel, and this is something you do have control over.

You can spend your day reading the news and being upset. You can keep yourself in a negative state of mind and prolong anger and frustration, or you can call a friend and spend time with them instead. In the end, you have no control over what is in the news, and regardless of whether you stayed upset that day or whether you laughed and joked with your friend, nothing in the world news changed.

However, one thing that did change was your emotions. And you did this because you focused on the things you did have some control over, which that day was connecting with your friend.

It's important for me to emphasize that this doesn't mean that you're giving in to the situation. It doesn't mean that you simply accept that this is how things are. If you can create change for yourself, then absolutely change it. If something angers you enough, then you can also choose to be a part of the change. You can choose to put yourself in a position that helps create the change you strive for.

But if you know there's absolutely nothing you can do, then change your focus. You have to change your focus because you're keeping yourself in a negative and unproductive state of mind if you continue to focus on the things outside of your control.

If you acknowledge that people suck, then how can you create positive emotions for yourself even though people suck? Now you have control. You could refocus your attention on projects that feel good to you. It could be about surrounding yourself with people who you know are positive for you and then maybe even recognize that not *all* people suck.

For you to be able to experience more positive emotions in a negative situation, you have to adapt. Take, for example, different species that have had to adapt to their circumstances over time; this is how they have survived extinction. Do you think that species would have evolved and survived if they encountered a new environment and simply rejected it?

It's not the strongest species that survives,
it's the most adaptable.

Say, for example, a species experiences flooding in their environment (and say for argument's sake that they have thought processes like humans do!). They're not going to evolve by saying that they shouldn't have to learn how to swim. They're not going to survive by saying that their land should still be dry, and they should still be able to continue living like they did before. This is not how they survive!

The way this species survives is that despite not liking their environment and despite not having much dry land anymore, they acknowledge that the water is now there so what can they now do to survive, even with this water in place?

This is how the species survives. This is how evolution works. And this has to happen to you too. It's the only way you can get your power back and create more positive emotions for yourself when you feel stuck.

The beautiful thing about this is all those things are within your reach! You're giving yourself full control back. So, the sequence is this - what are the stone-cold hard facts of your situation, regardless of whether you like them or not? What are the elements of that situation that you cannot control? Now with all these factors in place, what *is* in your control? What can you now do despite the parameters of your situation? And how can you move forward and adapt to your environment even with those factors in place?

27
ADJUSTMENT IS GRIEF

In this chapter, I want to talk about the fact that a lot of things that we go through, especially adjustments in life, are, in fact, grief. I know that when we go through grief, it's often associated with a loss through death. However, grief happens in so many forms.

Ultimately, grief is the need to adjust to something that's missing in your life. Whenever we don't like something, it's because we have a hard time adjusting to a new situation, whatever this situation may be. What this means is that by default, we're also experiencing the loss of something.

For example, if you move to a new place, it might be exciting because you're moving to a job you've wanted for a long time, and the whole experience can be very positive. But it also is accompanied by a feeling of loss because you may have built a solid social support system in the place you're leaving, and now you'll be missing your friends. You may also have had a good working relationship with your colleagues and boss, and this will be a loss also.

You'll be leaving a lot of things that have become familiar to you so even though you're experiencing an adjustment that is positive, there are still elements of loss present.

We're constantly adjusting to things because change is a part of life. That change also comes with a loss of something, no matter how small or big the adjustment.

When I talk to my clients about adjusting and how to adjust better to a situation, then often this looks very much like working through a grief process.

The end goal of grief is acceptance. You may be familiar with the five stages of grief, and the thing about the stages of grief is that it's not a concrete, structured thing. We don't work solidly and concretely in sequence through the five stages.

The first stage of grief is denial. At this stage, we haven't fully grasped what has happened and our situation hasn't sunk in yet. We don't want to accept that our loss is real. This stage has no fixed time limit on it. Depending on the situation and the individual resilience level, this stage can take a long time, or it can happen very fast.

The second stage of grief is anger. In this stage, you may ask yourself why this thing happened; it shouldn't have happened, it's not fair! In this stage, you're likely angry at the world, maybe angry at God, angry at the circumstances, and even angry at the person who died because they left you.

Even positive change can come with loss.

The third stage of grief is bargaining. This can be characterized by questions relating to the shoulda/woulda/coulda's. What if I'd done this instead of that? Would the person still be here? If only I'd done that! Bargaining can also be a plea to do everything right for that person to come back in some way.

The fourth stage of grief is depression. This is when we feel the loss. We're not in denial anymore, we know that life has to go on without the individual or the thing in our lives, and now we realize there's going to be a void in our life. There is going to be an emptiness there and knowing this fills us with sadness.

The fifth stage, which is the stage we strive for, is acceptance. And like I talked about in my previous chapter, it's about accepting the facts of the situation. It's not an acceptance in the sense of liking or agreeing with the situation, it's an acceptance of the reality of the situation.

Accepting the reality of the situation is how we can move in our lives. I talked a lot about this in my previous chapter, and experiencing adjustments in our lives works the same way.

The end goal of any kind of adjustment in our life is an acceptance that these are the new facts in our situation. It's only from this standpoint that we can move forward in our lives, but it's also about recognizing that when we're adjusting to a major change in our lives, and we feel stuck with it, it's because we haven't worked through the grief process.

I believe that when we start to approach major adjustments as grief, it can make us feel unstuck because it validates our emotions about the adjustment. For example, if you move to a new place because you've got a new and exciting job, maybe this job pays significantly more, and it's also way more in line with your long-term vision. The job is exciting, and you're moving to a city that's exciting, and all these great things are happening.

However, maybe you also feel sad, and you also feel loss because of all the things you're leaving behind. You may even find that once you've moved into your new place, you experience periods of struggle and difficulty because you miss your family and friends, and you may also miss your old job, even though you love your new job.

However, when you share this feeling of sadness with others in your life, quite often the initial response would be to quickly redirect this. They may respond with something along the lines of "Yes, but look what you've gained! You're in a much better place now, and you have all these great things in your life!"

These may all be true and valid; however, it doesn't acknowledge the loss. It doesn't validate your feelings regarding your loss and what you've left behind. It doesn't acknowledge the fact that there still may be things missing from your life even when you've gained a lot of things in life.

> Acknowledging grief helps people feel seen, not dismissed with a silver lining.

When it comes to adjustments, the loss that you're feeling is often dismissed, which makes you feel like there's no room for you to experience your emotions because the norm is to focus on the positives of your new situation. However, if we approach adjustment as a grief process, then that loss is also validated.

Now, if you experience periods of time where you're struggling, even though you have so many great things in life, you're still missing a lot of things you had in life and you're missing a lot of aspects of your old life. These two things - the loss of the old and the excitement of the new - can happen at the same time.

Instead of your feelings of sadness and loss being dismissed, now you're allowed to have these emotions because they are recognized and validated. You're allowed to experience missing your friends, and you're allowed to grieve that. You're allowed to feel your feelings while still acknowledging the positives in your life. You're not negating the positives in your life; you're allowing them to exist at the same time.

Many times, when clients come into my office and they're struggling with a situation, we talk about grief. We talk about how grief manifests in a lot of different ways.

For example, I had a client who was taking care of her dad full-time. There was some anger and resentment there because she couldn't move on with her own life because taking care of her dad was a full-time job. We could talk about working through this situation, but when you approach this situation from the perspective of grief, her feelings are very valid. She was grieving a life that she couldn't live.

It's remarkable how grief can manifest in so many ways. The obvious way is to experience grief through the death of someone you know. However, you can also grieve things. You can grieve a situation, and with my work with clients with addiction, I've seen that you can even grieve the loss of your substance.

In addition, you can also grieve something you've never had in your life before. For example, I had a client whose mom died when she was very young. She never knew her mom, and she had no memories of her mom as her mom died before she could start forming memories. However, she still grieved the fact that she never had a mom.

When you approach situations from a grief perspective, it can change your approach to how you work through the situation. For example, with my client who was taking care of her dad full-time, when we talked about her grief over the life she wasn't able to have for herself, the grief over lost opportunities, the grief over what her life could have looked like if she wasn't taking care of her dad, then she was able to see the extent to which grief was present in her life.

There was so much grief and loss there, even loss over things she never had in her life before.

You can grieve a person, a place, a plan, a season of life, or even something you never had.

Conversations about adjusting to new situations change significantly when approached from a grief perspective. Even positive things can be grief related. I've had conversations with another client who was very independent and needed a lot of her own space. She valued her alone time, and these things were important to her.

Throughout her life, she struggled with relationships and longed to be in a relationship where she felt connected and secure. She ended up meeting someone whom she was very compatible with and who she connected with. Over time, they moved in together and got married. She was happily married, but at the same time, she was struggling with not having her own space and time anymore.

We could talk about how to balance married life with having her own space and brainstorm how she could create space and time even while living with someone full-time. We could have conversations about how she could advocate for herself and how to ask for some more alone time, but the conversation changed focus when we approached it from a perspective of grief.

Now, we explored the loss of her free time and the loss of her independence. By approaching it from a perspective of grief, her feelings of loss were fully validated, and she was allowed to feel her feelings because, ultimately, it was a huge adjustment for her.

She was able to recognize that she was experiencing grief over her level of freedom while at the same time being happily married. Her feelings of loss were valid.

A solution-focused approach could have been helpful, but at the same time, it was not necessarily validating her emotional experience.

Focusing on solutions may have even felt somewhat dismissive because grief also involves allowing yourself to go through the process of feeling your feelings.

Unfortunately, the best way to get to the fifth stage of acceptance within the grief process is to go through it.

Going through the grief process means feeling your feelings and experiencing them. It means allowing yourself to cry and to be angry and to go through this emotional rollercoaster.

When we avoid or deny our feelings or rush through the steps by constantly distracting ourselves, then we're not allowing ourselves to go through the grief process. The only way to get to the acceptance phase is to go through the experience.

When things become more solution-focused rather than listening and experience-focused, it can feel dismissive of the feelings, and it doesn't allow the person to experience their grief. Like in the example of my client, who is adjusting to married life, that was a huge change for her.

I could try to encourage her to see all the positives in her situation and remind her that now she has found someone she can connect with, and this is what she wanted, etc., but it still doesn't validate the fact that she is having difficulty adjusting. It doesn't validate her feelings of loss.

However, when we approached her adjustment as grief, then she could sit with her feelings of loss. Her experience was validated, and she was allowing those feelings to exist.

It also doesn't mean her decision to get married was a bad decision. The beauty of validating people's emotions and experiences is that there's room for both. Both her feelings of loss of her independence and her excitement at being married to someone she connects with can coexist.

When we look at any version of adjustment as a grief process, then we're validating the loss within that adjustment. We're allowing ourselves those feelings and because we're validating that, we're giving it a place to exist. I believe once we've validated it, we can work through it and move through the grief process to come to a place of acceptance.

When our feelings are validated, that in itself can help resolve a lot of things. We don't always need solutions. Quite often, we need to be heard and it's important to be able to acknowledge that we don't need to be reminded of all the positive things all the time. Sometimes, we need our emotional experiences to be heard.

We also grieve very differently. Sometimes, it's impossible to gauge what to say to someone who is experiencing adjustment and loss; a statement that might be helpful and comforting to someone might be annoying and unhelpful to someone else.

For example, if someone is grieving a person through death and you tell them that you know that person is in a better place now, it might give someone comfort to know that they're not suffering anymore. This could be a helpful statement. However, for someone else, that same statement might feel incredibly dismissive because the loss is not being acknowledged.

We often have the tendency to want to distract the individual who is going through loss. We think that putting their minds in a different direction by focusing on something different can be helpful, and this could be so. However, grief is also about allowing that individual to feel sad.

Grief is about allowing yourself to feel upset and making room for those emotions. You wouldn't expect someone who's going through a painful period of grief to move on with their lives and to instantly be happy and to only focus on the positives in their life. Instead, you allow that person to grieve. It would be incredibly insensitive to expect that individual to quickly move on with their life without regarding their emotions about their loss.

If that person is hit with emotion and begins crying, you get it. You understand their response, and you allow it to exist. You wouldn't dismiss it and ask why they're crying, and hey, let's focus on the positives instead. No, you make room for the emotional expression.

However, when we're adjusting to a new situation, any kind of situation, this is quite often what we do. We dismiss the negative emotions and emphasize the focus on the positives. We do this because we don't acknowledge that there is a grief process involved with adjustment. By acknowledging grief, you're making room for sadness and loss, and you allow that person to work through their adjustment more effectively.

This theme of grief within adjustment is a recurring conversation with my clients. There are so many times when a client is in a situation where they are experiencing big changes in their life or they're struggling to adapt to a situation. When I recognize this, I often reframe their adjustment as grief and talk to them about the grief process and the five stages of grief.

I've found in my experience that when I approach adjustment issues as grief, my clients find this very helpful.

As a reader, if you can resonate with this and identify that you're going through major adjustments in your life, or you know that people around you are going through major life changes, even if those life changes are positive, then maybe it's good to be mindful that with those life changes comes a period of loss.

This could be the breakup of a relationship. Say, for example, you're in a relationship that you know, for the most part, is unhealthy, and it hasn't been good for you, but there have been good moments in the relationship as well. However, for the most part, it's been an unhealthy and even toxic relationship.

Then, you finally get the courage to break up with that individual, and you feel a sense of relief. You feel the freedom of being released from this individual, and you feel free from everything that was unhealthy about this relationship.

You know it was the right decision, and there's no question about whether you should or shouldn't have broken up with them. But maybe every now and then, you're reminded of something from the good times you had. Maybe you're reminded of the way you laughed so hard together or the way they acknowledged you in a moment, and suddenly, you miss that person so intensely.

Maybe you then feel an incredible sadness because, at that moment, the grief, the loss of that relationship hits you. Well, that's completely valid. Because the person was not healthy for you doesn't mean that you won't miss them.

It might be easier to constantly remind yourself that breaking up was the best decision and that you're in a much better place now, and even though you're correct, what you're also not doing is giving the feelings of grief and loss space to exist.

With any adjustment, any life change, good or bad, there's grief and loss attached to it. Of course, there are many different intensity levels of loss, but it's still grief and loss. Whenever you feel ungrateful for feeling bad in a situation in which you should feel excited, remind yourself that there's an element of grief you're experiencing there, too. When you allow these emotions to exist, you can now begin working through the grief process to come to a place of acceptance, thereby being able to move on and enjoy your life changes.

28
TRUST IN YOURSELF

Another common theme that I talk about with my clients, especially in the realm of anxiety, is the ability to trust in oneself. This becomes especially prevalent with people who worry about the unknown, who don't know if they're going to be able to deal with situations, or who don't know the outcomes.

Fear of the unknown is one of the most common types of anxiety. We often feel like we need to be in control of our circumstances or that we will only do well if we can anticipate every outcome.

> Fear of the unknown isn't the enemy.
> Distrust in yourself is.

It's not a bad thing to be prepared for different types of situations and to anticipate different scenarios; however, sometimes, the excessive worry about the future or the need to control or anticipate every single outcome slowly moves from being prepared to anxiety that is no longer productive.

We're all familiar with the phrase we'll cross that bridge when we get there, but I think an element that needs to be attached to this phrase is that you can also trust yourself to be able to cross that bridge when you get there.

You might not know what the outcome is, and you have no idea how things are going to work out, but you've also developed a trust in yourself that whatever comes your way, you can deal with it.

Sometimes, having this trust in yourself makes things a bit easier because I've also noticed that a lot of people don't feel like they can trust themselves. A lot of people don't feel like they can handle situations that haven't happened yet.

I've seen with many of my clients that if there's a situation with an unknown outcome, or if their thoughts go to the worst-case scenario, it is automatically accompanied by thoughts of it being too much, and they're not going to be able to deal with it. They often say they have no idea what they would do if the worst-case scenario happened.

What I also notice is that the thinking stops there. What they don't do is reflect and ask themselves, what if that *did* happen? What if this thing were to actually happen? How *would* I deal with that?

What I usually find is that they absolutely do have the capacity to deal with different situations. It's that they've never followed that thought through.

If a situation happens and you find yourself worrying about it excessively, you may tell yourself how you're not going to be able to deal with it and how it is going to work out. Now, you're thinking of all the awful outcomes and worst-case scenarios of your situation.

But what you're not thinking about is how you might deal with your situation. This situation now becomes two-fold.

First, the question to ask is how *would* you deal with a situation if you thought it would be a worst-case scenario? And second, it's about trusting that you will be able to deal with anything that may come up. It's about trusting that you do have the emotional strength to be able to handle any situation that comes along, and not only that, but you will also come out fine on the other end.

One very consistent observation I've made throughout the years is that people are incredibly resilient, and most people are far more resilient than they give themselves credit for.

One way that you can remind yourself of your ability to handle different situations is to remind yourself of different times in your past when things were very difficult. You remind yourself of times in the past when you struggled, you were going through a horrible situation, at the time it was a huge obstacle, and then identify where you're at today in relation to that difficult time.

This is when you will remind yourself of your resiliency and the fact that you did overcome that setback. It may have taken a while and it may have been a process, and that's okay. Sometimes, different life experiences take a while to overcome. The thing is, you did overcome it.

We all have experiences in our past that we've struggled with. We've all had experiences in our past that have been awful and painful. We've struggled, and we've gone through grief and anger and rejection and disappointment. We've all experienced these situations, and we've also overcome them.

Before those bad situations happened, we may have thought that we would never be able to handle situations like that, and at that time, it was the worst thing that could have happened. But we also found that somehow, we had the strength to overcome them.

I think it's also important to know that you don't need to know all the answers. You don't need to know what the obstacles are ahead of time. All you need to know is that you can trust yourself to overcome those obstacles when they do come up.

Say, I'm going to run a Spartan (obstacle course) race (AROO!). I have no idea what those obstacles are going to be. There may be new obstacles that I've never come across before, and there may be obstacles that I know I struggle with. There may be obstacles that I've never trained for. So, I'm worried about not being able to complete the obstacles, or I'm worried that I don't have the strength to complete the obstacles.

I can stress myself out this way, but instead of getting stuck in a loop of anxiety, I can ask myself if I can trust in myself to complete the obstacle. I can remind myself of times in the past when I have been able to overcome obstacles, thereby knowing I have the skill. I can also remind myself that if I don't complete the obstacle, I now have to do the penalty (thirty burpees! Yey!), and I know I can do thirty burpees.

So, I can either worry myself silly about the obstacle course and wonder if I'll be able to complete it, and what if I'm not strong enough or skilled enough etc. But then I also remind myself that the worst-case scenario is I do the penalty of thirty burpees, and I know I can do this. So worst-case scenario is I can move forward in the race.

Now, I can trust in myself that I am going to be able to complete the obstacle course, and this can help get me out of my anxiety loop.

This analogy happens in many different areas of life. A lot of things we experience in life are obstacles. We might not even succeed in completing the obstacle, but sometimes, it's not about passing or failing the obstacle but how we overcame it.

Whether you pass the obstacle or you don't, even if you fail the obstacle, can you trust in yourself that you can emotionally overcome whatever it is that you didn't accomplish? I already know that the answer is yes.

The answer is yes because you've done it many times in your life already. You don't need to know what the obstacle is. All you need to know is that you have the resilience and the strength to overcome it. You only need to know that you have the tools you need to draw on to be able to work through the outcome.

Maybe those tools include reframing different situations and learning how to gain back control. Those tools may include learning how to look at different situations with a new lens and using more effective problem-solving skills.

You can ask yourself if you have trust in yourself to apply these kinds of skills. If you're able to use these types of strengths in your life already, then you don't need to know the outcome of your difficult situation, and you don't need to know what lies ahead. You don't need all the answers because you have trust in yourself that you can use your skills when you need them.

If you find that you don't have trust in yourself, then this a very good time to do a few different things.

The first thing is to build up your toolbox of skills that will increase your resiliency in different situations. Maybe these are in-the-moment skills that can help you manage intense emotions, e.g., anger management skills. Maybe you find that your heightened anger or frustration gets in the way, and your impulsivity that results from these heightened emotions creates a lack of resiliency. When you recognize this, you can begin to increase your resiliency by learning to manage your intense emotions.

Another way to build resiliency is to create a healthier support system so that when you find that you're facing adversity and difficulty in your life, you have a good support system that you can draw on.

Having a healthy social support system makes going through difficult situations easier. Sometimes, when I suggest this to clients and encourage them to access their social support system during difficult times, a very common response is that they don't want to burden their friends with the things they are going through. However, I will often tell them that accessing a social support system is not about sharing their struggles with their friends, but sometimes it's about going out and having fun, chit-chatting about life, and having friends provide a healthy distraction for a while. Accessing a social support system is not about turning your friends into therapists!

Increasing resiliency could be about looking at how you can change your approach to a situation so that you can look at your situation from a new angle. I talked about this when I discussed reframing problems into challenges and identifying opportunities. When you face different obstacles in your life and there's a significant setback in your life, what are some ways that this obstacle can be reframed into a challenge?

There are many ways in which you can begin to develop trust in yourself. Another way to build trust in yourself is to remind yourself of your strengths from the past. You remind yourself of the times in the past when you have overcome your setbacks, even reminding yourself of how awful it felt at the time you were going through it. You may have felt at that time that things would never get better. You may remember thinking that what you were going through was the worst thing ever and that it's not ever going to get easier. And then you realize now that it did, and that you are in a better place, and that you did overcome your setback, even when you felt like you would never be able to.

When you remind yourself of all those times, then you also remind yourself that you do have the strength. You do have the tools to work through whatever situation comes your way.

> You don't need all the answers.
> You need faith in your ability to find answers when you need them.

The beautiful thing is that you don't need to know the outcome. You don't need to overwhelm yourself by trying to predict every outcome or prepare for everything. Doing so leads to paralysis and increased anxiety.

The only thing you need to be able to do is to have trust in yourself that you can overcome whatever it is that you're going to face in the future. So when you cross that bridge when you get there, you don't need to know what kind of bridge that will be. You don't need to know how high that bridge is or what it takes to be able to cross that bridge. All you need to know is that you know you have the tools to be able to make it to the other side.

ACKNOWLEDGMENTS

Special thanks to my husband, for tirelessly listening to me rant and dream aloud as I worked to bring this book to life.

I am forever grateful to my mom—my #1 fan and greatest cheerleader.

Deep thanks to Karen Waite and Susan Ince for being early readers and offering invaluable feedback that helped shape the content of this book.

To my editor, Stacey Smekofske—you were a breath of fresh air when I was hitting wall after wall. Without you, I'd still be trying to figure out half of what you so skillfully helped me accomplish. I am eternally grateful. This book would not exist without you.

Thank you to Tara Mayberry for the stunning cover and artwork that perfectly captured the heart of this project.

And lastly, to my clients—you were the inspiration for this book. It exists because of you.

ABOUT THE AUTHOR

Louise van der Eijk, LCPC, Ph.D., is a Licensed Mental Health Counselor with over 20 years of experience in the field. She holds certifications in clinical hypnotherapy and is trained in EMDR. Throughout her career, Dr. van der Eijk has worked across a broad range of mental health settings, including outpatient, community, residential, corrections, and crisis response. In addition to her clinical work, she has taught graduate-level courses, spoken at professional conferences and supervised clinicians working toward licensure.

Dr. van der Eijk currently maintains a private practice in Boise, Idaho. Outside the therapy room, she is a musician and serves as principal harpist with the Meridian Symphony Orchestra. She lives in Boise with her husband and their beloved four-legged companion.

www.ingramcontent.com/pod-product-compliance
Lightning Source LLC
Chambersburg PA
CBHW071431230926
51846CB00001B/189
9781968191009